The Readers' Advisory Guide to Horror

ALA READERS' ADVISORY SERIES

Serving Boys through Readers' Advisory

The Readers' Advisory Guide to Graphic Novels

The Readers' Advisory Guide to Genre Fiction,
second edition

Research-Based Readers' Advisory

The Readers' Advisory Guide to Nonfiction

Serving Teens through Readers' Advisory

The Horror Readers' Advisory:
The Librarian's Guide to Vampires, Killer Tomatoes,
and Haunted Houses

The Science Fiction and Fantasy Readers' Advisory:
The Librarian's Guide to Cyborgs, Aliens,
and Sorcerers

The Mystery Readers' Advisory:
The Librarian's Clues to Murder and Mayhem

The Romance Readers' Advisory:
The Librarian's Guide to Love in the Stacks

The Short Story Readers' Advisory: A Guide to the Best

The Readers'Advisory Handbook

The Readers' Advisory Guide to Street Literature

The Readers' Advisory Guide to Mystery,
second edition

The Readers' Advisory Guide to Horror

Becky Siegel Spratford

American Library Association

Chicago 2012

Becky Siegel Spratford coauthored the first edition of *The Horror Readers' Advisory: The Librarian's Guide to Vampires, Killer Tomatoes, and Haunted Houses.* She has been a readers' advisor since 2000 at the Berwyn (Illinois) Public Library. She graduated with honors from Dominican University's Graduate School of Library and Information Science in January 2001. She is currently an adjunct faculty member at the same school, teaching Readers' Advisory Service two semesters a year. Spratford also contributes content to NoveList, is a member of both the Adult Reading Round Table Steering Committee and the Horror Writers Association, and is the author of the blog *RA for All: Horror.*

Printed in the United States of America

16   15   14   13   12   5   4   3   2   1

Extensive effort has gone into ensuring the reliability of the information in this book; however, the publisher makes no warranty, express or implied, with respect to the material contained herein.

ISBNs: 978-0-8389-1112-9 (paper); 978-0-8389-9449-8 (PDF); 978-0-8389-9450-4 (ePUB); 978-0-8389-9451-1 (Mobipocket); 978-0-8389-9452-8 (Kindle). For more information on digital formats, visit the ALA Store at alastore.ala.org and select eEditions.

Library of Congress Cataloging-in-Publication Data
Spratford, Becky Siegel.
    [Horror readers' advisory]
    The readers' advisory guide to horror / Becky Siegel Spratford.—Second edition.
       pages   cm.—(ALA Editions' readers' advisory series)
    Includes bibliographical references and index.
    ISBN 978-0-8389-1112-9
    1. Fiction in libraries—United States. 2. Libraries——United States—Special collections—Horror tales. 3. Readers' advisory services—United States. 4. Horror tales, American—Bibliography. 5. Horror tales, English—Bibliography. I. Title.
    Z711.5.S68 2012
    026'.80883—dc23   2011043954

♾ This paper meets the requirements of ANSI/NISO Z39.48-1992 (Permanence of Paper).

ALA Editions purchases fund advocacy, awareness, and accreditation programs for library professionals worldwide.

CONTENTS

Series Introduction   vii

Preface: Why We Need Horror   ix

Acknowledgments   xi

1 **A BRIEF HISTORY OF HORROR**
How the Past Haunts the Present   *1*

2 **THE APPEAL OF HORROR**
Feel the Fear, Find the Readers   *13*

3 **HORROR 101**
A Crash Course in Today's Tales of Terror   *31*

4 **THE CLASSICS**
Time-Tested Tales of Terror   *49*

5 **GHOSTS AND HAUNTED HOUSES**
Home, Scream Home   *57*

6 **VAMPIRES**
Books with Bite   *65*

7 **ZOMBIES**
Follow the Walking Dead   *75*

8 **SHAPE-SHIFTERS**
Nature Morphs into Something Terrifying   *83*

9 **MONSTERS AND ANCIENT EVIL**
Cthulhu Comes Calling   *91*

10 WITCHES AND THE OCCULT
Double, Double, Toil and Trouble   *101*

11 SATAN AND DEMONIC POSSESSION
The Devil Inside   *111*

12 COMIC HORROR
Laughing in the Face of Fear   *119*

13 MOVING BEYOND THE HAUNTED HOUSE
Whole Collection Options for Horror Readers   *127*

14 SOWING THE SEEDS OF FEAR
Horror Resources and Marketing   *139*

Bibliography   153
Index   157

SERIES INTRODUCTION

Joyce Saricks and Neal Wyatt, Series Editors

In a library world in which finding answers to readers' advisory (RA) questions is often considered among our most daunting service challenges, library staff need guides that are supportive, accessible, and immediately useful. The titles in this series are designed to be just that. They help advisors become familiar with fiction genres and nonfiction subjects, especially those they don't personally read. They provide ready-made lists of "need to know" elements such as key authors and read-alikes, as well as tips on how to keep up with trends and important new authors and titles.

Written by librarians with years of RA experience who are also enthusiasts of the genre or subject, the titles in this series of practical guides emphasize an appreciation of the topic, focusing on the elements and features fans enjoy so advisors unfamiliar with the topics can readily appreciate why they are so popular.

Because this series values the fundamental concepts of readers' advisory work and its potential to serve readers, viewers, and listeners in whatever future space libraries inhabit, the focus of each book is on appeal and how appeal crosses genre, subject, and format, especially to include audio and video as well as graphic novels. Thus each guide emphasizes the importance of whole collection readers' advisory and explores ways to make suggestions that include novels, nonfiction, and multimedia, as well as how to incorporate whole collection elements into displays and booklists.

Each guide includes sections designed to help librarians in their RA duties, be that daily work or occasional interactions. Topics covered in each volume include:

- The appeal of the genre or subject and information on subgenres and types so that librarians might understand the breadth and scope of the topic and how it relates to other genres and subjects. A brief history is also included to give advisors context and highlight beloved classic titles.

- Descriptions of key authors and titles with explanations of why they're important—why advisors should be familiar with them and why they should be kept in our collections. Lists of read-alikes accompany these core author and title lists, allowing advisors to move from identifying a key author to helping patrons find new authors to enjoy.

- Information on how to conduct the RA conversation so that advisors can learn the tools and skills needed to develop deeper connections between their collections and their communities of readers, listeners, and viewers.

- A crash course in the genre or subject designed to get staff up to speed. Turn to this section to get a quick overview of the genre or subject as well as a list of key authors and read-alikes.

- Resources and techniques for keeping up-to-date and understanding new developments in the genre or subject are also provided. This section will not only aid staff already familiar with the genre or subject but also help those not familiar learn how to become so.

- Tips for marketing collections and lists of resources and awards round out the tools staff need to be successful working with their community.

■ ■ ■ ■ ■

As readers who just happen to be readers' advisors, we hope that the guides in this series lead to longer to-be-read, -watched, and -listened-to piles. Our goal is that the series helps those new to RA feel supported and less at sea and introduces new ideas, or new ways of looking at foundational concepts, to advisors who have been at this a while. Most of all, we hope that this series helps advisors feel excited and eager to help patrons find their next great title. So dig in, explore, and learn and enjoy the almost alchemical process of connecting title and reader.

PREFACE
Why We Need Horror

Readers love fantasy, but we *need* horror. Smart horror. Truthful horror. Horror that helps us make sense of a cruelly senseless world.

—Brian K. Vaughan[1]

It is hard to go anywhere in America today without confronting a vampire, zombie, or witch in some form or another. While Sookie Stackhouse teams up with vampires on TV and in the pages of Charlaine Harris's best-selling novels, zombies have stormed the world of Jane Austen's *Pride and Prejudice* bringing thousands of readers along for the ride, and Harry Potter has become the universal symbol of the witching world.[2] Although these creatures have gained mainstream traction in popular culture over the last twenty years, they have done so by slowly moving away from the world of horror where they were first conceived. Just the presence of a vampire, zombie, or witch on the pages of a novel or on the big screen no longer automatically makes the story "horror."

We are in the midst of a supernatural explosion in all fiction. If I had to name one trend in all popular fiction released in the last decade it would be the fact that supernatural elements have snuck their way into every genre. For example, readers can now find zombies populating the pages of political thrillers (Mira Grant's *Feed*), wizards running detective agencies (Jim Butcher's Dresden Files series), and ancient demons appearing as love interests (Sherrilyn Kenyon's *Night Pleasures*).[3] This trend is both a blessing and a curse for the readers' advisory librarian. We now have many more supernatural options for our patrons than we used to, but on the other hand, we have to pay much closer attention to *why* our patrons are seeking out paranormal scenes, plots, and characters in their leisure reading.

That is the big quandary which this book attempts to tackle head on. How does today's readers' advisor untangle true horror works from the larger mass of paranormal offerings? As the epigraph to this chapter reminds us, "we *need* horror." Readers have been drawn to works of horror fiction for centuries, and as readers' advisors, we have become their navigators. This book, then, becomes your map.

Advisors new to horror might find the prospect of the horror genre daunting, but remember, our horror readers are not monsters themselves, they just like to read about them. If you are worried about not knowing enough to field a horror-related RA question, don't be. Using this book, you can handle even the scariest of horror-related questions. I have included chapters on the history of horror, its appeal, and a "Horror 101" guide to the genre. There are chapters with annotated lists of horror novels categorized by their subgenres to help our patrons find the books that they would most enjoy, ideas on what other genres and formats our horror readers might enjoy, and tips on how to develop and market our horror collections—basically, everything we need to help our patrons find their next good scare.

Everything in this second edition has been updated and reevaluated, with new authors, trends, annotations, and suggestions. However, the biggest change is that this edition comes with a free electronic update—a blog that will continue to keep you apprised of the world of horror fiction specifically as it applies to librarians and their patrons.[4] No other horror resource is so tailored to your specific library needs.

So what are you waiting for? Enter if you dare . . .

NOTES

1. Brian K. Vaughan, introduction to *Locke and Key: Crown of Shadows,* by Joe Hill, illustrated by Gabriel Rodriguez (San Diego, CA: IDW, 2010).

2. Adapted from the Sookie Stackhouse novels of Charlaine Harris, *True Blood* currently airs as a series on HBO and is distributed on DVD by Warner Home Video. Harris's series begins with *Dead until Dark* (New York: Berkley, 2001). Seth Grahame-Smith and Jane Austen, *Pride and Prejudice and Zombies: The Classic Regency Romance—Now with Ultraviolent Zombie Mayhem!* (Philadelphia: Quirk Books, 2009). J. K. Rowling is the author of the Harry Potter series beginning with *Harry Potter and the Sorcerer's Stone* (New York: Arthur A. Levine Books, 1998). The Harry Potter films are distributed by Warner Home Video, Burbank, CA.

3. Jim Butcher's Dresden Files series begins with *Storm Front* (New York: Roc Books, 2000).

4. *RA for All: Horror,* www.raforallhorror.blogspot.com, is produced and maintained by Becky Spratford as the online home of this text.

ACKNOWLEDGMENTS

Before we begin, I want to thank the people without whom this book would not be in front of you right now. First, to Michael Jeffers and his wonderful staff at ALA Editions, thank you for having the faith in me to go it alone for this second edition. This book was greatly improved by the comments, insights, and friendship of series editors Neal Wyatt and Joyce Saricks. Specifically, there were days when I was simply stuck, and just a short conversation with Joyce refocused me with renewed vigor. I also am grateful to Nancy Bent of the La Grange (Illinois) Public Library and Anne Slaughter of the Oak Park (Illinois) Public Library who agreed to read drafts, made comments, and shared their insight. This book also benefited from the generosity of my colleagues at the Adult Reading Round Table, who allowed me to try out my rough draft on a live audience in September 2010.

I am also indebted to my colleagues at the Berwyn (Illinois) Public Library, specifically our director, and my former coauthor, Tammy Clausen, whose support never waivers even after eleven years together, and Briana Perlot, who offered me technical and emotional support. But it is the "Dream Team" of our Readers' Advisory Department, led by Kathy Sexton, that makes showing up for work a joy. We are a cohesive unit, completely devoted to finding our patrons their next good read.

I also want to acknowledge those who helped me by letting me take time away from working for them while I concentrated on finishing this book. Susan Roman, dean of the Graduate School of Library and Information Science at Dominican University, and Katherine Johnson at NoveList both let me take a leave of absence from my various responsibilities and never pestered me about when I would return. The breathing room was greatly appreciated.

And, finally, to the people who had to live with me on a daily basis throughout this process, deal with my distractedness, and spend entire days talking about nothing but zombies, vampires, and werewolves—my husband, Eric, and my children, Samantha and Nathaniel—I could not have finished this book without your patience, love, and support.

1

A BRIEF HISTORY OF HORROR
How the Past Haunts the Present

> I read that every known superstition in the world is gathered
> into the horseshoe of the Carpathians, as if it were the centre
> of some sort of imaginative whirlpool; if so my stay may be
> very interesting.
>
> —Bram Stoker, *Dracula*[1]

In 1974, Stephen King published *Carrie,* and the world of horror fiction changed forever. However, although Stephen King may be the most accomplished and best-known horror writer ever, he was not the first to write in the genre. Horror has a long and interesting history. Arming yourself with knowledge of this history will assist you as you guide your patrons through the dark passages of horror. Although most of this book will focus on the present state of horror, I am a big proponent of the saying that in order to know where you are now (or even where you are going), you need to know where you have been.

In that spirit, I offer this very brief history of horror. By no means is this review meant to be the definitive word on the genre. For that, you can turn to the many full-length books dedicated to the subject.[2] This is a history for the general librarian, the person sitting at the service desk and helping leisure readers each and every day. This is the history you need to know, the bullet points, major themes, and changes over time—the history that will let you see the whole picture so that you can feel comfortable talking about the genre to your patrons.

The history of horror is complicated. Horror, like romance, has been slow to gain legitimacy in the literary arena, partly because it has been the victim of fuzzy and overlapping genre boundaries. Horror has moved from being a literary element within the pages of science fiction, the serial-killer thriller, and dark fantasy novels to having its own defined genre. The merging of horror into other genres continues, and under the umbrella classification of speculative fiction, we often still find horror partnered with fantasy and science fiction. Regardless of our tendencies to blend genres, horror fiction contains elements that differentiate it from other genres. The most prominent of these is the author's intention of creating a frighteningly uneasy atmosphere. This emotional punch feeds readers' powerful voyeuristic desire to explore the dark, malevolent side of humanity in an imaginative framework. This feeling, a mainstay of the horror novel, gets at the heart of why readers have been drawn to these stories for centuries.[3]

The rest of this chapter is a peek into what horror was and how it evolved into what it is today—a genre I define as a story in which the author manipulates the reader's emotions by introducing situations in which unexplainable phenomena and unearthly creatures threaten the protagonists and provoke terror in the reader.[4]

THE GOTHIC NOVEL

In 1765, Horace Walpole published the first Gothic novel, *The Castle of Otranto*.[5] This publication is widely considered to mark the beginning of the horror genre. Horror elements had been present in literature before this, of course, but after this date there was an explosion of Gothic writings with recurring themes and plot lines characterized by "an emphasis on portraying the terrifying, a common insistence on archaic settings, a prominent use of the supernatural, the prescience of highly stereotyped characters, and the attempt to deploy and perfect techniques of literary suspense."[6] These are stories of ancient castles, dark passageways, and ghosts. Typical plots involved an evil villain pursuing a young woman, and although she is confused and scared, she ultimately triumphs, and the villain is exposed.

Emphasizing atmosphere over plot development, the Gothic novel became synonymous with excess and exaggeration, portraying the terrors of the haunted house, vampires, werewolves, and soulless monsters unleashed on society. Classic examples include Matthew Lewis's *The Monk* (1796), which shocked readers with its account of rape and torture, and John Polidori's *The Vampyre* (1819), one of the first novels to feature such a being.[7] But arguably the most influential Gothic novel of this era was Ann Radcliffe's *Mysteries of Udolpho* (1765). Set in the sixteenth century, this popular novel told the story of the orphaned Emily St. Aubert, who upon her parents' deaths was made the ward of her aunt, Madame Cheron. The aunt marries the sinister Italian Count Montoni, who carts Emily off to a dilapidated castle in the Apennines and plots to steal her inheritance. Emily must find a way to escape.

Although the Gothic period is said to have ended with the publication of *Frankenstein* in 1818, the Gothic tradition continued to influence some of our best-known classics such as the Brontë sisters' *Jane Eyre* and *Wuthering Heights,* as well as Jane Austen's *Northanger Abbey.* The Gothic influence is also evident in the writings of nineteenth-century American authors such as Edgar Allan Poe, Nathaniel Hawthorne, and Henry James. Today we see novels written in the Gothic tradition by authors as varied as Joyce Carol Oates, Alexandra Sokoloff, and Charlaine Harris. Box 1.1 lists some Gothic authors of note.

Box 1.1 *Gothic and Gothic-Influenced Authors*

Charlotte Brontë	Joseph Sheridan Le Fanu
Emily Brontë	Matthew Lewis
Wilkie Collins	Edgar Allan Poe
Charles Dickens	John Polidori
Nathaniel Hawthorne	Ann Radcliffe
E. T. A. Hoffman	Horace Walpole

THE ENLIGHTENMENT AND ITS INFLUENCE

At the close of the eighteenth century, social critics and intellectuals of the time were uniquely situated to witness the rise of science and technology as well as what some perceived to be the social and moral decline of the West. The Enlightenment brought an increased knowledge of the natural world and a weakening of religious dogmas. People began to question what happened after death as well as the existence of God. The works and lectures of T. H. Huxley, a Darwin defender, serve as great examples of the issues and ideas of the era. Huxley believed that science emerged when the human brain had evolved to a certain level of complexity.[8] If wisely used, the marvels of science would allow civilization to reach new heights, and humanity would evolve even further. But, he warned, humans had begun as lowly creatures and still had a primitive side to their nature.

Motivated by this dark side, people could use science to enslave others and manufacture weapons of destruction. The use of science for good, or evil, and humankind's evolutionary process and primal fears became central themes for the horror genre. The fear that technology and science were taking over our lives was real, and it manifested in writings about the terrible things science could do in the hands of the wrong people.

The Enlightenment and the ideas it spawned were debated by intellectuals and social thinkers for decades, but the first novel to explore these ideas was Mary Wollstonecraft Shelley's *Frankenstein* (1818), which gave readers the first mad scientist who attempted to circumvent God and create life in man's image. The results were disastrous for Dr. Frankenstein, and readers were left with a lasting warning about the consequences of playing God.

Another example from this era is *The Strange Case of Dr. Jekyll and Mr. Hyde* (1886) by Robert Louis Stevenson, which delved into the mental health of man, the structure of personality, and the fear that we can unknowingly become our own worst nightmare. The possibility of transforming ourselves only to discover that our alter ego is a monster is as terrifying now as it was back then. The grandfather of science fiction, H. G. Wells, was also experimenting with the new scientific discoveries of the time, focusing on the scarier aspects of these ideas and extrapolating them into a frightening future. In *The Island of Doctor Moreau* (1896), Wells specifically warned of what the world could expect if it failed to control the outrageous pace of scientific progress. On the surface, Moreau is a mad scientist, in the mold of Dr. Frankenstein. He heartlessly contours the shapes of his innocent animal subjects in a blind search for forbidden knowledge. But what he is really doing is far worse. Moreau has set himself up as the divine creator of vivisected creatures who in turn view him as their god. At a time when scientific progress seemed to be supplanting religion, these books were the scariest stories imaginable.

The nineteenth century came to a close with the most recognizable horror novel of all time. With the publication of *Dracula* (1897), Bram Stoker created a novel that has now become synonymous with the vampire motif. *Dracula* is one of the best-selling novels of all time, has never been out of print, and, in fact, has only become more popular over time.[9] Stoker's vampire was not the first to ever appear in literature, but in this epistolary novel, Stoker created the stereotype of the vampire as an aristocratic bloodsucker who preys on young women.[10] Stoker's image of the vampire has become so pervasive in popular culture that Dracula is now the most frequently portrayed character in all horror films.[11] As Brian

Stableford has noted, "No other novel of any kind has ever stamped out an image so firmly and so decisively."[12] To most people, Count Dracula is not only *the vampire,* he is the definition of horror. See box 1.2 for a list of authors from this era.

Box 1.2   *Key Horror Authors of the Enlightenment*

Mary Wollstonecraft Shelley	Bram Stoker
Robert Louis Stevenson	H. G. Wells

THE GHOST STORY AND BEYOND

The early years of the twentieth century were the golden age of the ghost story.[13] M. R. James set the tone and developed many of the genre classifications of the ghost story, a subgenre that is still very popular. In a ghost story, characters are haunted by a spirit and are forced to battle both the spirit and their own inner demons in order to survive the ordeal.[14] Authors such as Edgar Allan Poe, Henry James, Edith Wharton, H. G. Wells, Anne Rice, and Stephen King have all experimented with ghost stories, leaving a rich tradition of the haunted. For a longer list of the ghost story writers of this golden age, see box 1.3.

Box 1.3   *Ghost Story Authors*

Ambrose Bierce	Henry James
Algernon Blackwood	M. R. James
Robert W. Chambers	Arthur Machen
Walter de la Mare	Oliver Onions
W. W. Jacobs	

However, the most influential horror writer of the early twentieth century was the eccentric hermit H. P. Lovecraft. Lovecraft influenced a number of other writers of his time and beyond with his stories about human encounters with ancient beings of horrific and alien appearance who occasionally intrude into our world from other dimensions. These works are called the Cthulhu Mythos stories, and many of them were published in the popular magazine *Weird Tales.*[15] Both Lovecraft's stories and the magazine attracted a cult following. In fact, after Lovecraft's death, writers continued to publish Cthulhu-inspired stories. Even into the twenty-first century, new tales of Cthulhu continue to appear every few years, and you can find YouTube feeds and entire websites devoted to Cthulhu themes.[16]

THE PULP ERA: 1930–1973

What Lovecraft started took on a life of its own, and a new era of horror literature became popular. Sometimes referred to as the pulp era, this period produced the beginnings of modern horror as we know it. Readers had been primed by Lovecraft's outrageous and terrifying stories, and after his death in 1937, they craved more. Authors such as Ray Bradbury, Shirley Jackson, and Richard Matheson who grew up reading Lovecraft began their popular and influential careers writing horror novels and stories during this era. Their work is now widely considered among the best genre fiction ever produced and is still being mined by the film industry for popular movies.

In fact, a trip to the movies is the next big step in the history of horror literature. Since cinema's infancy, horror novels and films have shared themes and characters, such as vampires, zombies, ghosts, and werewolves, and the popularity of horror movies helped to pull horror novels into the mainstream consciousness. During the 1930s and '40s, Universal Pictures produced classic, atmospheric horror films based on earlier novels. In 1931, Bela Lugosi played his signature role as Dracula, and Boris Karloff brought Frankenstein to the big screen. Karloff showed his theatrical abilities again in 1932 in the portrayal of Imhotep, a 3,700-year-old Egyptian brought back to life in *The Mummy.* Then in 1941, Universal made the quintessential werewolf film, *The Wolf Man,* with Lon Chaney Jr. and Bela Lugosi. The impact of these films on popular perceptions of these monsters, invented first in the pages of novels, was enormous. The movies expanded and added to the original creations, providing visual images of the classic stories, images that persist. Since that time, the horror movie and the horror novel have been irrevocably linked.

In the 1940s and '50s horror fiction was struggling. There was less time for leisure reading in general with the country focused on the war effort, but the movies brought back the genre, which in turn reignited an interest in horror novels. The 1960s brought popular retellings of Poe's Gothic tales to films starring Vincent Price. However, the most influential horror film of the decade was undoubtedly George Romero's 1968 classic zombie film, *Night of the Living Dead.* Not only did Romero set the stage for an increase in the explicit gore in horror films, but he also set the standard for all zombie stories, in all formats, forever after.[17]

Although *Night of the Living Dead* began its life as a movie, two notable horror novels from this era were also made into hugely popular and critically acclaimed motion pictures: Ira Levin's *Rosemary's Baby* (1967) and William Peter Blatty's *The Exorcist* (1971). The former is about a woman impregnated with Satan's son, while the latter is about the battle for the soul of a young girl who is possessed by an ancient demon. Specifically, *Rosemary's Baby,* both the novel and Roman Polanski's 1968 film version, is considered one of the classics of the horror genre and instrumental in its evolution.[18] The film was nominated for numerous awards, including two Academy Awards.[19] *The Exorcist* did even better. When the film came out in 1973, it was the highest grossing film of all time until it was surpassed by *Jaws* in 1974.[20] *The Exorcist* was nominated for ten Academy Awards, including Best Picture, and won two, including one for Blatty's work on adapting his novel for the screen.[21] The legacy of these two novels lives on through their films, drawing new readers to their pages year after year. These classic horror novels are also extremely important because of their place at the end of an era. Consult box 1.4 for a further list of the major horror authors of the first seventy-five years of the twentieth century.

Box 1.4 *Major Twentieth-Century Horror Authors, 1900–1973*

Peter Benchley	Roald Dahl	H. P. Lovecraft
A. G. Birch	August Derleth	William March
William Peter Blatty	Daphne du Maurier	Richard Matheson
E. F. Bleiler	L. Ron Hubbard	E. Hoffman Price
Robert Bloch	Shirley Jackson	Donald Wandrei
Ray Bradbury	Fritz Leiber	Henry S. Whitehead
Hugh Cave	Ira Levin	

Things in the world of horror, however, were about to change forever, as a new author took the reins as horror master.

THE DAWN OF MODERN HORROR: 1974–1999

As well as things were going for horror fiction up to this point, everything changed in 1974 when Stephen King published his first novel, *Carrie*. Not only did this event mark the beginning of horror's modern era, but King has also become one of the most important authors in America.[22] After King began publishing, all horror novels would come to be judged by the high standard he has set throughout his still vibrant career. The 1970s also introduced readers to Anne Rice's vampire, Louis de Pointe du Lac, and his confessions in the best-selling *Interview with the Vampire*. Rice went on to romance her readers with many novels of vampires, witches, and mummies for over twenty years and served as the inspiration for today's immensely popular paranormal titles. Dean Koontz also began his long domination of the best-seller charts with his genre-bending, horrific thrillers in the 1970s. The combination of these three powerhouses moved horror novels into the spotlight; it seemed that just about everyone in America was reading a book by one of these authors. Even more amazing, all three are still widely read, even Rice, who has not written a new horror novel in over a decade.[23]

As we moved into the 1980s, King, Koontz, and Rice were still leading the charge, but Clive Barker entered the horror scene, intensifying the sex and violence in the genre. Barker's novels and stories also fed the growing fascination with slasher films—such as the *Halloween* and *Nightmare on Elm Street* series—by adding one of his own in the *Hellraiser* films, featuring the terrifying sadomasochist villain, Pinhead.

Inspired by the writings of these stalwarts, many new horror writers found a readership and prospered during this time. (See box 1.5 for a more complete list.) In fact, horror became so in demand that in 1984, one of its more popular authors, Robert McCammon, used an interview with *Publishers Weekly* to publicly declare his desire for a writers' association strictly geared toward the "needs of fellow writers of fear."[24] Working with fellow novelists Dean Koontz and Joe Lansdale, McCammon formed the Horror Writers of America in 1986. The association began issuing the highest honor in horror literature, the Bram Stoker Award, in 1987. The group has since changed its name to the Horror Writers Association and continues to be the leading voice of the horror writing community, promoting the work of its members, issuing internationally recognized genre awards, and educating the world about horror.

The 1990s brought more of the same with King, Koontz, and Rice ruling the genre, but as a result of their intense popularity, a new genre was beginning to emerge. Led by the literary novels of Neil Gaiman, dark fantasy gained popularity as we approached the new millennium. With the sales of horror books staying high and the Horror Writers Association working to promote horror, readers wanted more. Just as past horror writers borrowed from other genres, now fantasy writers were looking toward horror to inject new life into their work. Stephen King even tried his hand at dark fantasy, writing the bulk of his popular Dark Tower series during this decade.[25]

Box 1.5 provides a longer list of influential horror authors from 1974 to 1999.

Box 1.5 *Major Horror Authors, 1974–1999*

Clive Barker	Joe Lansdale	John Saul
Ramsey Campbell	Richard Laymon	Dan Simmons
Douglass Clegg	Bentley Little	Michael Slade
Tananarive Due	Brian Lumley	Brian Stableford
John Farris	Graham Masterton	Peter Straub
Christopher Golden	Robert McCammon	Whitley Strieber
Charles Grant	Christopher Moore	F. Paul Wilson
Jack Ketchum	Kim Newman	Chelsea Quinn Yarbro
Stephen King	Tom Piccirilli	
Dean Koontz	Anne Rice	

A NEW MILLENNIUM: 2000–PRESENT

The draw of dark fantasy continued to overshadow much of what would be considered true horror as the 2000s began. Popular paranormal series like Jim Butcher's Harry Dresden series, Charles de Lint's Newford books, and Charlaine Harris's Sookie Stackhouse series dominated the decade, often overshadowing true horror.[26] Although these dark fantasy series use common horror monsters or dark, unsettling atmospheres, or both, in their stories, their main appeal is not to induce fear. Rather, their focus is more grounded in the traditional fantasy appeal of creating a magical landscape, albeit a darker one. But the biggest difference between this century's popular dark fantasy and pure works of horror is the fact that in dark fantasy, the monsters are often the heroes, while in horror, monsters remain monsters.[27]

The attention paid to dark fantasy does not mean that horror novelists have not been producing work of note. The new millennium has seen a reemergence of the paperback horror novel similar to the pulp novels of the mid-twentieth century. Horror writers have also been among the first to embrace new technology, using blogs and e-books in large numbers. One popular horror writer, Scott Sigler, takes the use of technology one step farther by releasing his novels in serial form via free podcasts before they come out in print. Horror has also moved into the graphic novel format with much success. And a true new horror master of the twenty-first century, Joe Hill, has emerged as a best seller in the vein of his father, Stephen King, to lead the genre into a new century. Box 1.6 lists some of the most influential horror novelists of the 2000s.

Box 1.6   *Major Horror Authors of the Twenty-first Century*

Gary Braunbeck	Sarah Langan	Harry Shannon
Max Brooks	Deborah LeBlanc	Scott Sigler
John Everson	Edward Lee	John Skipp
Greg Gifune	Jonathan Maberry	Bryan Smith
Joe Hill	Robert Masello	Alexandra Sokoloff
Brian Keene	Joe McKinney	Jeff Strand
Nate Kenyon	Weston Ochse	
Michael Laimo	Sarah Pinborough	

TIME TO MOVE ON . . .

Horror has evolved over time into its own best-selling genre by borrowing themes and techniques from the past as well as by forging new territory and expanding its boundaries. Today's horror novelists understand this. References to Poe, Lovecraft, Stoker, and many of the pulp writers pop up frequently in horror books. Readers respect this, and they will also expect you to have a basic understanding of the genre's deep traditions.

For those who are interested in delving further into the books upon which the history of the genre is based, I suggest familiarizing yourself with the twenty-one books Robert Weinberg suggests that all horror writers read for themselves in his article, "What You Are Meant to Know: Twenty-One Horror Classics."[28] The list is annotated to help you to better understand each title's place within the larger context of the history of horror literature.

But now it is time to leave the past behind and enter the world of horror in the twenty-first century.

NOTES

1. The epigraph is taken from the first chapter of Bram Stoker's *Dracula*, Project Gutenberg, www.gutenberg.org/ebooks/345 (accessed September 7, 2011).
2. For a more detailed history I suggest you begin with David Punter, *The Literature of Terror: The History of Gothic Fiction from 1765 to the Present Day* (New York:

Longman, 1996). I also like David Pringle, *The St. James Guide to Horror, Ghost and Gothic Writers* (Detroit: Gale, 1998). You can use both books' extensive bibliographies to guide any further research into the history of horror literature.

3. Chapter 2 will provide a more detailed discussion of the appeal of horror.

4. This definition is further discussed in chapter 2, "The Appeal of Horror: Feel the Fear, Find the Readers."

5. The 2001 Penguin edition of *The Castle of Otranto* has been edited and includes an introduction and notes by Michael Gamer.

6. Punter, *Literature of Terror,* 1.

7. The 2002 Oxford University Press edition of *The Monk* has an introduction by Stephen King.

8. T. H. Huxley, *The Advance of Science in the Last Half-Century,* Project Gutenberg, www.gutenberg.org/ebooks/15253 (accessed October 8, 2010). A full listing of Huxley's works can be found at www.gutenberg.org/browse/authors/h#a595.

9. Nina Auerbach and David Skal, eds., *Dracula,* Norton Critical Edition (New York: W. W. Norton, 1997), preface.

10. Lawrence J. Trudeau, ed., *Twentieth-Century Literary Criticism,* vol. 238 (Detroit: Gale/Cengage Learning, 2010), 256.

11. *Guinness Book of World Records,* www.guinnessworldrecords.com/news/2007/10/071031.aspx (accessed October 10, 2010).

12. Brian Stableford in Pringle, *The St. James Guide to Horror,* Literature Resource Center database (Gale/Cengage Learning; accessed October 10, 2010).

13. Michael Stuprich, ed., *Horror* (San Diego: Greenhaven, 2001), 21.

14. Chapter 5 contains a lengthy discussion of the ghost story, its history, and suggested titles to read.

15. *Weird Tales* has been resurrected recently and can be accessed at http://weirdtales .net/wordpress/ (accessed October 13, 2010).

16. Examples include an ongoing Cthulhu-inspired graphic novel series titled Fall of Cthulhu written by Michael Alan Nelson, beginning with *The Fugue* (Los Angeles: Boom! Studios, 2008). See also the various collections of new Cthulhu stories, such as John Pelan and Benjamin Adams, *The Children of Cthulhu: Chilling New Tales Inspired by H. P. Lovecraft* (New York: Ballantine, 2002). A Google search for Cthulhu brings up almost 4 million results, and Cthulhu is represented close to 4,000 times on YouTube (accessed October 10, 2010).

17. In Mira Grant's zombie-filled novel, *Feed* (New York: Orbit, 2010), the protagonist tells the reader that Romero is a godlike figure to her society. His film, she argues, saved their lives when zombies really did come back from the grave. In this fictional world, the zombie of Romero is kept alive for scientific study as a tribute to his importance.

18. In his seminal work on the genre, *Danse Macabre* (New York: Everest House, 1981), Stephen King includes a discussion of both the novel and the film in chapter 9, "Horror Fiction."

19. *Rosemary's Baby,* http://en.wikipedia.org/wiki/Rosemary%27s_Baby_%28film%29#Awards_and_honors (accessed October 13, 2010).

20. *The Exorcist,* http://en.wikipedia.org/wiki/The_Exorcist_%28film%29 (accessed October 13, 2010).

21. Ibid.

22. I'm not the only one who makes these claims. In 2003, King was awarded the National Book Award for Distinguished Contribution to American Letters by the National Book Foundation. Recipients of this award are chosen because they have "enriched our literary heritage over a life of service, or a corpus of work" (www.nationalbook.org/amerletters.html).

23. For more about King and Koontz, see chapter 3 of this text.

24. The Horror Writers Association, "A Shockingly Brief and Informal History of the Horror Writers Association," www.horror.org/aboutus.htm (accessed October 13, 2010).

25. Stephen King's Dark Tower series begins with *The Gunslinger* (New York: Signet, 1982).

26. Jim Butcher's Dresden Files series begins with *Storm Front* (New York: Roc Books, 2007); Charles de Lint's linked Newford books begin with *Dreams Underfoot* (New York: Orb, 2003); Charlaine Harris's Sookie Stackhouse series begins with *Dead until Dark* (New York: Ace Books, 2008).

27. Chapter 13 addresses the dark fantasy/horror debate in more detail.

28. In Mort Castle, ed., *On Writing Horror: A Handbook by the Horror Writers Association,* rev. ed. (Cincinnati, OH: Writer's Digest Books, 2007).

TITLE/AUTHOR LIST

Carrie, by Stephen King

The Castle of Otranto, by Horace Walpole

Dracula, by Bram Stoker

The Exorcist, by William Peter Blatty

Frankenstein, by Mary Shelley

Interview with the Vampire, by Anne Rice

The Island of Doctor Moreau, by H. G. Wells

Jane Eyre, by Charlotte Brontë

The Monk, by Matthew Lewis

Mysteries of Udolpho, by Ann Radcliffe

Northanger Abbey, by Jane Austen

Rosemary's Baby, by Ira Levin

The Strange Case of Dr. Jekyll and Mr. Hyde, by Robert Louis Stevenson

The Vampyre, by John Polidori

Wuthering Heights, by Emily Brontë

2

THE APPEAL OF HORROR
Feel the Fear, Find the Readers

Horror is not a genre like mystery or science fiction or the western. It is not a kind of fiction meant to be confined to the ghetto of a special shelf in libraries and book stores. Horror is an emotion.

—Douglas Winter[1]

WHAT IS HORROR?

A basic understanding of why readers crave horror fiction can be found in the epigraph to this chapter: "Horror is an emotion." Readers love horror for the way it makes them feel. It is the emotions that these novels elicit—the fear, anxiety, uneasiness, the pure terror—that bring readers back again and again. That emotional pull is also what makes horror so personal. What scares one reader may not even faze another. Therefore, it is important to have a strong working definition of horror that can capture the range of the genre while giving you a framework for determining what is and isn't horror.

In this book I have defined horror as a story in which the author manipulates the reader's emotions by introducing situations in which unexplainable phenomena and unearthly creatures threaten the protagonists and provoke terror in the reader. That is our starting point, and everything will build on this definition. If you need to refer to it at any time, see box 2.1.

Let's more closely examine this definition, starting with the manipulation of emotion. Horror readers want to be scared. We will worry about how the author accomplishes this momentarily, but the first thing you

---

Box 2.1   *Definition of Horror*

Horror is a story in which the author manipulates the reader's emotions by introducing situations in which unexplainable phenomena and unearthly creatures threaten the protagonists and provoke terror in the reader.

---

need to understand is that regardless of the way the author produces feelings of fright, be it through graphic scenes of violence, a psychologically unsettling situation, or the creation of an uneasy atmosphere, it is the emotional pull of the story that makes it a satisfying horror novel. If you take only one thing away from this book, it should be an understanding of this simple fact: horror is an emotion.[2] The author must set an uneasy tone from page one and sustain it throughout the work, even up to the last line, in order for the story to be a successful work of horror.

Let us now consider the means by which authors create this emotional punch. In order for a book to be considered horror, the author must introduce unexplainable phenomena or unearthly creatures or both, setting them loose to run amok and stalk the protagonists. The threat must slip the bounds of the realistic and enter a realm that is the opposite of our known reality, one where authors are free to imagine that vampires, ghosts, and zombie plagues exist. These otherworldly events and monsters must threaten both the characters in the story and the reader turning the pages.

This feature is what makes horror horror—the monster, force, or villain that is stalking our heroes, raising our pulse, and forcing us to read with the lights blazing cannot be of our real world. Horror fans love that they truly believe in the monsters in their books while they are reading, but are happy to leave them on the page and return to the real world when they finish. For some readers, the threat in horror must be of a supernatural origin, but increasingly, horror authors are using scientific elements (such as a zombie virus) as the spark behind their threat. The result is still the same. These are creatures and phenomena set within a frame that is outside our known world; as they stalk the characters, the reader is terrified and loving every minute of it.

Therefore, the fundamental feature of a horror novel is that it must terrify the reader and do so with a pervasive sensibility. The reader needs to feel uneasy from the first page, even before any kind of monster is introduced. This unsettling feeling, coupled with the otherworldly threat, provokes pure terror—the desired, and inescapable, emotional response all horror fans seek. The rest of this chapter will take this definition of horror and show you how to use it when helping horror readers.

WHAT IS NOT HORROR?

Before we go any farther, it must be stated that the working definition of horror used in this book excludes many titles that readers enjoy and may discuss as horror titles. It does so deliberately in order to help you navigate the increasingly common blending of genres and more clearly understand what readers are really saying when they tell you they want a horror title. Getting the genre distinctions right is critical when working with readers, as failing to do so will very often lead you and your reader to books that do not satisfy. For example, if a patron tells you she likes horror and goes on to discuss her love of the Sookie Stackhouse novels, you need to know that she likes paranormal fiction, not horror.[3] Patrons don't need to understand the distinction, but you do. If you use patrons' classification terms only, in this case "horror," and do not understand what they are really asking for, you will naturally use horror resources to find a book, and that book is likely to be a mismatch. Let's explore some of the most popular types of books that readers may call horror but that are actually not part of the genre.

Paranormal

You cannot work at a public library in America today without knowing that paranormal fiction is hugely popular. In order to better educate librarians on the appeal of paranormal fiction, Neil Hollands moderated a panel discussion at the 2009 American Library Association Conference titled, "Things That Go Bump in the Stacks: Whole Collection Advisory for Paranormal Fiction."[4] Hollands began the program with a great overview of paranormal fiction by explaining that although it encompasses almost every genre, the overall grouping of paranormal fiction and urban fantasy is useful to explore because all the books share common elements. Paranormal fiction, Hollands explained, blends contemporary fiction with an alternate paranormal world. It can appear in any genre, not just horror.

Hollands then recounted how paranormal fiction got its start in horror fiction, but that horror novels were different in one big way. In horror, traditionally, the paranormal characters are less sympathetic. They are the "bad guys" and, as a result, the biggest threat to the heroes. In today's paranormal fiction, the paranormal characters are not only sympathetic, they are quite often the heroes of the story themselves.

This character shift is a huge distinction between the genres and matters greatly to readers—even if they have never thought through their enjoyment enough to articulate it to you during an RA interview. Again, think about the readers of Harris's Sookie Stackhouse books. They love that Sookie is in love with two different vampires, that she is friends with shape-shifters and werewolves, and that she herself is a fairy. There are scary supernatural people in this series, but the main ones are the heroes and the romantic leads. Compare this to *The Passage*, a horror novel by Justin Cronin, in which vampires are the bane of the surviving humans' lives. There is nothing sexy or romantic about them. They are destroying the world. And it is the heroes' fear of the vampires, and their desire to defeat them, that propels the story.

Serial Killers

Although paranormal fiction is slowly becoming its own genre, there are other types of books that some readers will refer to as "horror." The ones that are as close as you can get to a horror novel, without truly being one, are serial-killer thrillers. Everything about the serial-killer book is horrific: it is creepy and scary from page one, and the monster stalking the protagonist is very, very evil, but this monster is not an unearthly creature; he or she is 100 percent human. Serial-killer books are very popular with many horror fans, but this approval does not make them horror novels.

Traditional Monsters Revolt

Novels featuring vampires have also been moving out of the horror genre in droves. Beginning with the publication of *Interview with the Vampire* by Anne Rice in 1976, vampires have slowly been morphing into the romantic leads of the books in which they appear. This transformation is most obvious in the popular Twilight and Sookie Stackhouse series.[5] Vampires in popular literature are often more sexy than scary these days. However, the evil vampire may be making a comeback, so watch out![6]

Not only vampires have flown the horror coop; many series have popped up in the last ten years with traditional horror characters, such as demons, witches, and werewolves, whose main intent is not to provoke fear in the reader. These stories can range from dark fantasy to mystery to romance to a mixture of all three. Some of the most popular of these series are Jim Butcher's Dresden Files, Kelley Armstrong's Women of the Otherworld, and Julie Kenner's Demon-Hunting Soccer Mom.[7]

When I stress that these books are *not* horror, I am not blind to the fact that many of them will appeal to horror readers. In fact, chapter 13 of this book, "Moving beyond the Haunted House: Whole Collection Options for Horror Readers," is dedicated to just this issue. But again, in order to get the clearest picture possible of what horror *is,* you need to see it next to what it is *not.* To that end, I will offer a side-by-side comparison of two popular fiction titles that both feature zombies; however, one is clearly horror, while the other is a political thriller.

Horror versus Not Horror

Sparrow Rock by Nate Kenyon follows six teenagers who survive a nuclear bomb explosion in an underground bunker. As they await rescue, things go from bad to worse. First, they may not have been in the bomb shelter by accident; second, mutant bugs begin turning everyone into zombies. Should they stay locked underground or attempt to make it on the outside? This heart-pounding, edge-of-your-seat horror novel is all about the fear—the fear of being sole survivors, the fear of the unknown above, and finally, the fear of being infected or killed or both by the zombies. And this unease continues until the last page, as our protagonist makes it through the first obstacle only to be faced with an unknown threat. The reader knows who won the battle but has no idea who, or what, will win the war.

Feed by Mira Grant, on the other hand, also features zombies, but it is a political thriller more in the mold of a Brad Meltzer or David Baldacci book.[8] It is set in a near future where the cure for the common cold mixed with the cure for cancer has created a zombie problem. However, this mishap is just the backdrop. The crux of the story concerns a group of bloggers who, while following a presidential candidate, uncover a huge plot, which goes up to the highest levels of government, to use the zombie virus to put a different man into the presidency. Yes, there are zombies here, and lots of them, but the draw of this novel is the action-packed story of the good guys taking down the bad guys. The reader does not come away from *Feed* feeling unsettled as with *Sparrow Rock;* rather, the reader feels triumphant and fulfilled after completing *Feed.*[9]

THE APPEAL OF HORROR

Enough with the quibbling. It is time to get to the heart of why your horror-loving patrons crave the genre so. In *Danse Macabre,* Stephen King presents a social scientific analysis–cum–personal memoir of his love for works of horror. One of King's most memorable comments about horror comes quite early in the book: "The work of horror really is a dance—a moving rhythmic search. And what it's looking for is the place where you, the viewer or the reader, live at your most primitive level."[10] This dance metaphor is a great place for us to begin thinking about horror readers and their devotion to the genre.

In *Readers' Advisory Service in the Public Library* (ALA Editions, 2005), Joyce Saricks set the readers' advisory standard for getting to the heart of why readers enjoy a certain book. Terming this quality *appeal,* Saricks argued that librarians could use descriptors about a book's pacing, characterization, story line, frame/setting, tone/mood, and style/language to understand the feel of the book. Using the framework created by Saricks, I will both describe and rank the main appeal factors of the horror genre to aid you when working with readers. If you need a cheat sheet to the appeal factors when helping readers, I have included them in an outline form in box 2.2.

Tone and Mood

The central appeal of horror is the feeling it generates. There is no question that the tone and mood of a horror book are the most important appeal factors for horror readers. More than in any other type of literature, the horror novel's ultimate objective is to scare by manipulating the reader's emotions. It gives a voice to our fears, delivering the dark emotions of panic, chaos, destruction, aversion, and disgust that we horror readers find uncompromisingly intriguing.

It is atmosphere above all else. Often the most terrifying moments are achieved through subtle suggestion rather than through a series of shocking scenes and brutality (although that can happen too). A well-created atmosphere is integral to a successfully appealing horror story. More important than character and plot development, we need to feel the fear created by the author. We need to feel the approaching danger in the background details as well as in the actual attacks. Horror goes after a visceral response in the reader, attacking us in our guts. A deeply sinister mood must be created to make the story unsettling enough to be believable. In

---

Box 2.2 *Horror Appeal Factors*

Tone and mood

- Provoke terror
- Give voice to our fears
- Create uneasy atmosphere

Characters: Sympathetic; we care about them.

Pacing: Builds steadily to frantic conclusion

Language and style

- Lots of adjectives but still frank and colloquial
- Can be quirky to build unease
- Flashbacks common

Story line: Common themes and issues

- Unexplainable phenomena and unearthly creatures threaten
- Coming-of-age
- Safe exploration of the dark side of humanity
- Place where readers can face own fears
- Escape from life's real horrors
- Validation of belief in the supernatural

Frame and setting: Vary, but authors will often use a specific frame or setting and focus on it in detail in order to enhance the tone and mood of the story.

---

fact, the best horror novels create a sense of fear and dread that follows the reader off the page. Fans want to feel anxious and uneasy even after closing the book.

Characters

Although the atmosphere of horror is the key appeal to the genre's readers, the order of importance for the rest of the appeal factors will vary from reader to reader. In my experience, however, characters come next. Horror readers want characters that they care about. If we do not like the protagonist, we will also not care that he or she is endangered.

To create these sympathetic characters, horror writers often spread the point of view around in their novels. We can see how different characters are reacting to the situation, we get to know multiple characters more deeply, and we come to care about them all. However, even when the point of view shifts, one true hero always rises to the occasion. Another technique horror authors use to create sympathy is to include human villains, or foils to the protagonists. There is often one human character whom the reader does not trust, who is not good and just, and whom the reader may even root against.

Pacing

Although there is no standard pacing for a horror book, all horror stories need to build in intensity. They will start out at a leisurely pace, but they move more quickly as the action increases and the dread builds. As the fear and terror are ratcheted up, so too is the pacing. By the end, what may have begun leisurely has become relentless. In fact, I dare any fan to put a horror book down for more than five minutes in the last third. It is just about impossible. And if you can manage it, you will probably need to keep the lights on as a precaution.

Language and Style

The language of a horror book is quite distinct. Horror novels are liberally filled with adjectives—many, many adjectives: adjectives that describe smells, sounds, and sights, adjectives that allow readers to feel the fear with all their senses. These adjectives are essential in creating the atmosphere mentioned earlier. However, this copious use of adjectives does not make horror novels flowery or dense in any way. Overall, the writing is frank and colloquial. This is everyday, accessible language describing extraordinary occurrences in great detail.

The style of horror novels also supports the mood. Authors often employ quirky style choices to highlight the unease in horror novels. Diary entries, fake documents, e-mails, lost papers, and frequent shifts in point of view are all common in horror stories. But the most common stylistic choice is the use of the flashback. Flashbacks serve two purposes in the horror novel. First, they help to underscore the dark tone by going back to a time when things were much better. The juxtaposition makes the current situation seem even worse by comparison. The flashback acts as a magnifying glass, intensifying how bad things have become. Second, flashbacks provide a break in the bleak hopelessness of the current story line; going back to happier times allows the reader to breathe easily if only for a few pages. Even the most ardent horror fan could use a break as the unease and dread build to near bursting levels.

Story Line

Horror readers care about the actual plot much less than the previously listed appeal factors. This preference does not mean that the story line is not important; in fact, the story line is instrumental to a horror reader's enjoyment. It simply means that readers may not verbalize plot elements to you in the readers' advisory interview. This omission makes knowing common themes even more imperative if you want to have successful interactions with your horror readers.

First, let's remember our horror definition: all horror is set in a world where unexplainable phenomena and unearthly creatures constantly threaten. Readers have to be willing to suspend their disbelief. As I discussed at length earlier, without these otherworldly elements, the story is not horror.

Many common themes and issues pop up in horror stories, the most prominent being the coming-of-age theme. In every horror novel, the protagonist not only is battling physical demons but also has to "grow up" and overcome his or her personal demons, to rise to the occasion and triumph. This struggle is a huge appeal factor in the horror story that cannot be overlooked. These are flawed protagonists, who are average in every way; many are even misfits of some type. Readers are drawn to the hero's similarity to themselves. They, reluctantly at first, rise to the occasion, defeat the monster, and become surer of themselves.

A powerful voyeuristic thrill compels readers to explore the malevolent, dark side of humanity with forbidden decadence, and horror novels are a way to do this safely. These novels provide a harmless way to acknowledge the wickedness within our own psyches and take a small peek into this illicit world. Tangentially, horror also allows its readers to face their own fears. We are all scared of something, and reading a story of others overcoming monsters, witches, or mummies empowers us to face our own fears. As bad as our worst fear may be, it cannot be worse than staring down a pack of zombies. In a similar vein, horror is also a great escape from the real horrors of life. Fiction in general is often noted for its ability to let the reader escape the real world, but horror specifically seems to be a popular antidote to hard times. As King notes in *Danse Macabre*:

> Horror movies and horror novels have always been popular, but every 10 to 20 years they seem to enjoy a cycle of increased popularity and visibility. These periods almost always seem to coincide with periods of fairly serious economic and/or political strain.[11]

We have been at war and under economic strain for many years now, and horror novels and films have not been this popular since the 1980s. The rise in the popularity of horror today may reflect readers' desire to escape current economic and political difficulties.

Finally, horror story lines are appealing to many because they validate belief in the supernatural. Horror feeds off this natural curiosity by creating situations in which unexplainable phenomena and unearthly creatures are the norm. Everyday life can be a series of mechanical or logical events, or both, but many people look for more out of life. Still others are looking for answers or explanations for the problems and tragedies in their own lives. The supernatural becomes an alluring solution in these situations. One of the most common supernatural topics tackled in the genre is life after death. Ghosts, spirits, vampires, zombies, and mummies all come back from the dead. Even though these life-after-death scenarios usually involve the risen being wreaking havoc on the people and places in the novel, it is oddly comforting to the reader to have his or her fears about what happens to us after we die answered in some tangible way.

Frame and Setting

A horror novel can be set just about anywhere; the only requirement is that the setting allows for the characters to be isolated from the larger populace in some way. Popular examples are islands, storms that cut off communication with the outside world, deserted old homes, apocalyptic times, or being taken prisoner. Contrary to popular belief, a horror novel does not need to be set in a small, rural town. There is horror set everywhere, from cities to the country, foreign and domestic, North and South. If there is a specific setting that appeals to your patron, rest assured there is a horror novel taking place there.

Horror novels can feature any background frame; it really depends on the writers' outside interests. Popular frames are medical and scientific ones. As mentioned in chapter 1, humans have always been wary of technological advances taking over too much of our lives, and those with more scientific knowledge are inherently scary. But there are also authors like Jonathan Maberry who are personally accomplished in another field, such as martial arts, and include details of this interest in their novels. Other authors have interests in popular culture, music, movies, comics, and more. These interests show up in their novels. Sometimes a specific frame is included to help lighten the mood, such as in Brian Keene's *Castaways*, which is organized around the frame of a reality television show.

Appeals Applied

The best way to understand how these appeal factors are realized in a novel is to take a closer look at a specific text. In this case, I am going to discuss two popular novels from 2009, the aforementioned *Castaways* by Brian Keene and *The Unseen* by Alexandra Sokoloff. Both were well received and written by two of today's best horror writers; however, they are on opposite ends of the spectrum. Both are horror, both take advantage of the same appeal factors, but both would probably please completely different readers. Let's see how each author uses common horror appeal factors to different ends.

First, let's review the plot of each book. In *Castaways*, a television crew and contestants in a *Survivor*-esque reality show are literally caught in a fight for their lives—the island they have been left on is populated by an indigenous tribe of bloodthirsty monsters! It is a grisly page-turner. In contrast, *The Unseen* is based on the true-life researchers and students from the Duke University Parapsychology Lab in the 1960s who went to study poltergeists in a haunted house. No one returned unscathed. Today, Professor Laurel MacDonald and three others return to the haunted home in the hopes of getting some answers, but are they prepared for what they will find?

Next, let's look at the tone and mood for each. Both books set up an uneasy mood from page one by beginning with a tense and anxious situation. *The Unseen* begins with a dream sequence (although the reader does not know it is a dream until the scene is completed) in which Laurel is making her way down a dark hallway heading toward something terrible. We feel the dread, the fear, and we are unsure of what to expect. In *Castaways*, on the other hand, the book opens with a challenge in which the participants in the reality show have been dumped out at sea and have to swim back. Our protagonists are struggling to stay afloat, and we feel their panic as they gasp for breath.

These novels both do an excellent job of using the very first scene to set up a nightmarish mood. Also, both step back from this extreme unease after the initial scene and begin setting up the plot. The respite is small, however, because these opening scenes are very powerful. The mood is set but not forgotten; it stays with the reader and keeps him waiting for what is going to go wrong next. And let me tell you, what goes wrong next is way worse, but seasoned horror readers are anticipating this, too.

Keene and Sokoloff use their characters in classic horror fashion. Keene sets up a story with three reluctant hero protagonists. Two men and a woman, who are "good guys," lead the charge against the devolved, humanoid monsters that are attacking them. One person is also the comic relief, which is good because this is a bloody and violent book. There is also a very bad and selfish contestant whom Keene allows to evade a gruesome end until the very last pages of the book. As our heroes escape, our villain finally gets his due, and I dare any horror reader not to be rooting for the monsters at that moment.

Sokoloff takes a different tack. She concentrates her entire story on Laurel. Laurel is trying to get over a very bad breakup, delving into the paranormal secrets in her family while trying to advance her career. The reader is invested in Laurel. We cheer for her as she begins to figure out some of the secrets of the Parapsychology Lab, and we trust her when things begin to go terribly wrong at the haunted house and she must save everyone. Sokoloff does introduce another researcher in opposition to Laurel, and the reader is not meant to trust him, but our hatred of him is not as intense as in *Castaways*. We are simply wary of him throughout the novel.

So far the books sound fairly similar, but when we get to pacing, the differences between these books increase. Both novels use the classic horror pacing of slowly building to a frenetic, breakneck speed. However, with Keene's multiple protagonists and a mean human villain, the slow build only lasts for about the first third of the novel. Then, the action comes at you nonstop for the final two-thirds of the book. The pace is relentless as the action is constantly switching. There are chase scenes, blood and guts, grisly deaths, vivid rape scenes, and daring escapes. We even get a glimpse into the psyche of the monsters. Sokoloff on the other hand, with her focus on Laurel and her internal struggles, builds the story and the tension for the first two-thirds of the book. By the time Laurel and her team get to the haunted house, the reader is bursting, ready for the action. But even then, Sokoloff gives us a little and then pulls back again. It is not until the last third of the novel that the pace increases, and then it is relentless. The break in the action does not come until the reader closes the book.

Both novels also use language and style to their advantage. *The Unseen* introduces old reports from the 1960s into the story and uses flashbacks frequently to show how Laurel got to this point in her life. The language is formal, academic, controlled, and clean to reflect the narrator; there are no "blood and guts" in this story. The adjectives describe spooky storage rooms, odd occurrences at the house, strange sounds, and creepy feelings. *Castaways* is quite the opposite. Here the language and style reflect the tongue-in-cheek premise of the book—a show that sets up a fake survival premise and then turns into an all-too-real fight for life. The language is crass, blunt, and, at times, almost campy. There are graphic scenes of brutal slayings and disturbing rape scenes, but there are also comical scenes of utter incompetence. This is a graphic pulp story with a sense of humor, and the language reflects that.

In terms of story line, both plots require that the protagonists "come-of-age"; this change is imperative in each story. All the heroes come to terms with their personal shortcomings and defeat the monsters they are facing, both the supernatural and the personal. As part of this coming-of-age theme, while the protagonists face their personal demons, readers are implicitly forced to look inside themselves to face their own fears. *The Unseen* introduces the dark side of humanity through a few villains, but its focus is much more on validating a belief in the supernatural, since the premise of the book is an attempt to study paranormal activity through science. But *Castaways* flips these appeals. The entire focus of this novel is on the dark side of humanity. The monsters that are attacking the castaways are human, or at least they used to be. They are a race of devolved humans who have turned into terrible abominations. You cannot have a more blatant comment on our species' tendencies toward the dark side than the situation Keene creates. Finally, both novels provide their readers with an escape from the true horrors in their own lives; the full-force haunting that Laurel and her crew are subjected to at the end of *The Unseen* and the horrific circumstance on the island in *Castaways* are much worse than anything we are facing in the "real world."

Both novels also feature an isolated frame: a haunted house, set apart in the country, and an island, isolated even further by a terrible storm. Obviously, the extreme isolation of these settings enhances the overall tone of the novels. The academic frame in *The Unseen* makes the story a bit more subtle and psychological. Things are thought through and analyzed, and attempts are made to scientifically explain the paranormal activity. This frame makes the utter inexplicability of the final scenes even more intense; the reader is terrorized without any graphic violence. *Castaways* uses its satirical frame to help temper its graphic use of blood and guts. Without the reality television frame, *Castaways* could be too much to take. This is not a book for the weak-stomached, but it is more appealing to a wider audience than are some other visceral horror stories because of its frame.

HORROR TRENDS

The appeal of horror is fairly constant, but there are some trends right now that are worth mentioning. I have highlighted these trends in box 2.3.

Box 2.3   *Horror Trends*

Horror elements are creeping into all genres of fiction.

Zombies versus vampires.

Horroresque series are incorporating strong elements of horror and other genres, especially apocalyptic-thrillers and paranormal romance.

No character is safe!

Comic horror is hugely popular.

Horror films are being released all year long, not just around Halloween.

You would have to be living under a rock to not know that vampires and zombies are all the rage in every type of fiction—actually, in every type of media. As a result of this ubiquity, people are less frightened by these formerly horrific characters. It takes a different emphasis and a lot more atmosphere building if an author wants to shock readers with a zombie or vampire story. Also, as mentioned earlier in this chapter, horroresque series are popping up everywhere. Most notably in paranormal stories or apocalyptic-thrillers, horror characters are becoming stars of their own long-running series, ensuring that this fad may be here to stay.

Probably the most surprising trend in horror over the last decade challenges what many readers hold as a sacred truth in horror stories: no one is safe anymore. Horror readers used to be assured that no matter what happened, no matter how many people died during the course of the novel, the main character, at least, would make it through alive. This outcome is no longer a given. I have seen horror books in which main characters die, in which the narrator dies before the end of the book, even in which everyone dies. These are not fringe books either. I am talking about mainstream titles.[12] This trend adds a new level of anxiety and fear to every horror story. Once readers have seen the protagonist die in one novel, they fear that it could happen in another.

Right now, comic horror is also doing very well. Initially I thought it might be a fad, but many of the comic titles appear to have traction, thus moving the subgenre into the trend category. Chapter 12, "Comic Horror: Laughing in the Face of Fear," is devoted to this popular subgenre, but for now, understand that a lot of readers are looking for horror with a sense of humor, specifically, horror that can tell a compelling, terror-provoking story while still poking fun at itself, as in S. G. Browne's *Breathers: A Zombie's Lament.*

While many horror readers are laughing their way through their books, horror filmmakers are taking advantage of a renewed interest in all horror and releasing horror movies all year long. Previously, if you wanted to see a horror movie in the theater, you could go only in the six weeks around Halloween. In the last few years, however, horror films have been popping up in theaters throughout the year. Their popularity has also led to more horror movies being watched at home, again at any time of the year. How does this affect you, the librarian? Well, with more people seeing horror films in general and at unpredictable times, the more your patrons are being exposed to the genre. Exposure often spawns interest. Readers will be ripe for horror suggestions and may even be seeking more horror titles than usual. This trend will also be discussed in more detail in chapter 14, "Sowing the Seeds of Fear: Horror Resources and Marketing."

WORKING WITH READERS

There are a lot of issues to take into account as you consider the pleasures of horror. As you saw with *The Unseen* and *Castaways*, novels can use the same common horror appeals with widely differing results. These novels are on opposite ends of the horror spectrum, yet both came out in 2009, both were popular, and both were well reviewed. Sokoloff and Keene expertly set up a menacing atmosphere from page one, but it is how they then choose to tell their story, sustain the dread and uneasiness, and apply the appeal factors that makes them so different. These horror novels will not necessarily satisfy the same reader. The question now is, how do you match these books with the correct reader?

Taking the appeal issues outlined in this chapter and seeing how authors use them is the first step toward helping your readers. You need to use this information to narrow down which books the patron would most enjoy at this moment. When interviewing readers that you think might enjoy horror, it is best to start with the definition of horror (see box 2.1). If they are receptive to horror, your next step is to go to box 2.2 and use the bullet points there to guide you through the readers' advisory transaction. Ask questions about each area of appeal in order to get a sense of which specific horror titles your readers would enjoy.

Obviously, you cannot conduct a successful readers' advisory interview without knowing more about specific books to suggest to each type of reader. Relax, that is my job. The rest of this book will break down specific authors and titles with a focus on the appeal of these works. Plot will be considered, but I will focus on what readers find most appealing about these titles and authors. Once you are primed by my descriptions, you should try out a few of the authors or titles for yourself. No matter how helpful this text can be, it is no substitute for reading a horror novel yourself. This book will give you many suggestions for where to start your own exploration of the dark side. Later, I will also have some suggestions on how to organize and market your collection to potential horror readers. By thinking about how to help your horror readers before they come to your desk, you will serve their leisure reading needs more efficiently and effectively.

But Wait . . .

You can be the biggest horror fan yourself or a great student of the genre and still come up against some difficult patrons. Readers have their quirks and specific needs. With horror I see this individuality in the form of a preference for certain types of speculative threats. A reader will claim not to care what she is reading as long as it has, for example, werewolves in it. This reader wants werewolves and only werewolves. Asking her about the level of gore she wants in her books or whether a menacing atmosphere is paramount is not important here. To help with this type of reader, beginning with chapter 4, I have included lists of books based on the horror subgenre they fall into, with annotations that will help decipher their appeal.

The key to helping any reader is to understand what is most compelling about a specific book. I have given you the key to begin unlocking your horror patrons' passion for the macabre. Think in their terms. You may not want to feel unsettled when reading for fun, but they do. You don't have to share their passion in order to help; you just need to understand why they love feeling the fear and use it to help them find their next good read.

NOTES

1. Douglas E. Winter, introduction to *Prime Evil: New Stories by the Masters of Modern Horror* (New York: New American Library, 1988).
2. In *The Readers' Advisory Guide to Genre Fiction,* 2nd ed. (Chicago: ALA Editions, 2009), Joyce Saricks groups the major literary genres in categories, placing Horror in part 2, "Emotions Genres," along with Gentle Reads, Romance, and Women's Lives and Relationships.
3. Sookie Stackhouse is the main character in both the series of novels by Charlaine Harris, beginning with *Dead until Dark* (New York: Berkley, 2001), and the HBO television series titled *True Blood.*
4. Hollands has continued to make his presentation available for free online at http://readersadvisory.org/paranormal.html (accessed October 14, 2010). My discussion of his talk is based on these documents and my notes on the program, which I attended. My notes were approved by Hollands himself, and you can view them as well as his comments at http://raforall.blogspot.com/search ?q=things+that+go+bump+in+the+stacks.
5. Stephenie Meyer is the author of the popular young adult series beginning with *Twilight* (New York: Little, Brown, 2005).
6. A longer discussion of vampires can be found in chapter 6, which provides an annotated list of vampire horror, and in chapter 13, which discusses the whole collection options for horror fans.
7. Jim Butcher's Dresden Files series begins with *Storm Front* (New York: Roc Books, 2000); Kelley Armstrong's Women of the Otherworld series begins with *Bitten* (New York: Plume, 2003); Julie Kenner's Demon-Hunting Soccer Mom series begins with *Carpe Demon* (New York: Berkley, 2005).
8. Brad Meltzer's *The Book of Fate* (New York: Warner Books, 2006) is a wonderful read-alike suggestion for *Feed.*
9. Because of a major plot twist in *Feed,* there is a bit of sadness after the victory, but there is not fear.
10. Stephen King, *Danse Macabre* (New York: Everest House, 1981), 17–18.
11. Ibid., 40.
12. *Spoiler alert!* In the best-selling novel *The Ruins* by Scott Smith (New York: Knopf, 2006), every single character succumbs to the killer plant that stalks them throughout the story.

TITLE/AUTHOR LIST

The Book of Fate, by Brad Meltzer
Breathers: A Zombie's Lament, by S. G. Browne
Castaways, by Brian Keene

Feed, by Mira Grant
Interview with the Vampire, by Anne Rice
The Passage, by Justin Cronin
The Ruins, by Scott Smith
Sparrow Rock, by Nate Kenyon
The Unseen, by Alexandra Sokoloff

3

HORROR 101
A Crash Course in Today's Tales of Terror

A basic truth: People love monsters. Whether those monsters
are vampires, ghosts, werewolves, demons, or shapeless blobs
that devour everything in their path makes little or no difference.

—Karen E. Taylor[1]

By this point, you have read about the evolution of horror and now have
a working definition of the genre for the new millennium. Also, using the
appeal guidelines detailed in chapter 2, you can now more easily identify
horror novels and have a knowledgeable conversation with your horror
readers. The terms, common tropes, and general feel of horror should be
much less scary to you. Still working with the definition of horror today
as a story in which the author manipulates the reader's emotions through
the use of a speculatively created threat all with the intended goal of provoking terror, it is time to identify the biggest authors in the genre today.
These are the men and women who have embraced this definition, mas-
saging horror's most endearing appeals into their plots, ultimately creating works that have captivated readers. Don't worry, these authors don't
bite; they only write about creatures that do. This chapter is a blueprint of
the genre, its heaviest hitters, their start-with titles, and author read-alike
options to help guide your readers to new tales of terror. The structure of
this chapter also makes it easy for you to use as a ready reference guide
to the genre. The authors are presented in categories: The New Heads of
Horror, Old Guard, Pulp Kings, and Ladies of the Night. In each category, I will describe the appeal of each author and give you a "start with"
suggestion. The result is a stand-alone chapter that chronicles the most
popular horror authors today. It is a document you will come to rely on as

you work with readers. It is your crash course in horror. Finally, for those librarians looking to delve further into the genre, this chapter could be used as the jumping-off point for a longer genre study.

THE NEW HEADS OF HORROR

The two authors who best define the current state of popular horror fiction, accurately reflecting its nuances, genre-blending tendencies, and format-crossing realities while still putting fear at the forefront of their works, are Joe Hill and Jonathan Maberry. These authors are the reigning kings of terror; their stories, novels, graphic novels, and nonfiction set the current high-water mark for the genre. Any discussion of horror today must begin with them.

Joe Hill

Joe Hill is the leading creator of twenty-first-century horror. He writes novels, short stories, and graphic novels. As the son of America's greatest living horror writer, Stephen King, Hill had a head start on his career path, but he has taken his good fortune, worked on crafting his own style, and emerged with his own unique talent.

Hill's novels and stories always feature extremely flawed but genuinely likable protagonists who are forced to confront their dark sides as they battle an evil supernatural being. A Hill tale also sets the stage with a menacing atmosphere from the first lines. For example, in *Horns,* the story begins as Ig is waking up after a rough night; in fact, he can't really remember much of what happened. He goes to the bathroom and sees himself in the mirror. There are horns growing out of his head! Before the book has gone past page one, Ig and the reader are already uneasy, unsettled, and just plain scared of what is going to come for the next 370 pages. Hill does this in every book and story he writes: he grabs our attention, makes us anxious, and dangles the promise of even worse to come, all on the first page.

Today's readers are also drawn to Joe Hill because he mines their modern lives for fear, such as in *Heart-Shaped Box,* where an old-fashioned haunted house story is predicated on the purchase of a ghost off the Internet. But even with these modern touches, Hill produces old-fashioned chills. His graphic novel series, Locke and Key (illustrated by Gabriel Rodriguez), follows the three Locke children as they deal with their father's murder, their alcoholic mother, and a supernatural being who is stalking them. These are typical twenty-first-century American kids; they listen to iPods and text each other, but they also live in a creepy, isolated old house, filled with keys that can do magical and dangerous things. Although the protagonists live in modern times, the feud between their family and the supernatural being out to collect all the keys and destroy them has been going on for generations. Hill captivates readers with his ability to use the best of the time-tested horror traditions while injecting a shot of the new to keep things freshly frightening. The results are realistically chilling.

Hill captures the cross-genre tendencies in all of today's fiction by often incorporating into his works some of the aspects of the suspense novel and many dark fantasy tropes. For example, Ig may become the devil, but he is also using his newly emerging powers of darkness to track down his girl-friend's killer. Hill also writes short stories to go along with his novels and graphic novels, thus capturing even more readers. Finally, Hill's original, chill-inducing works contain an average amount of violence for the genre. There are blood and guts, but the violence is never gratuitous.

Readers new to Joe Hill should start with his Bram Stoker Award–winning *Heart-Shaped Box.*[2] Jude Coyne is an aging rock star, obsessed with the supernatural. On an Internet auction site, he buys an old suit that is said to come with a ghost. Thinking the story a joke, Coyne buys the suit and ends up getting much more than he bargained for. The ghost has a personal vendetta against Coyne, and the two spend the novel in a struggle over his past mistakes and, ultimately, his life.

Fans of Hill's writing who want to read more may also enjoy the horror novels of Jonathan Maberry, Stephen King, and Peter Straub, who are also highlighted in this chapter. These horror authors all write character-centered horror that is rooted in the reader's real-life experiences. The chilling suspense of Tom Piccirilli is also a great choice for Hill readers. Piccirilli began as a horror writer and has continued to keep a supernatural element in his works. Like Hill, Piccirilli has flawed but sympathetic protagonists, placed in frightening situations, with modern details. Another whole collection option for Hill fans is the psychological suspense of Peter Abrahams. Like Hill, Abrahams excels at leading his protagonist into a bad situation, while readers squirm as they watch it all spin out of control. The ultimate question with both of these authors is whether the protagonist will make it out alive. It is important to note here that both Piccirilli and Abrahams are *not* horror authors, but they would still greatly appeal to fans of Hill.

Jonathan Maberry

Jonathan Maberry may not be as much of a household name as Joe Hill, but there is no doubt he is just as important. Maberry is a busy, award-winning author. He writes traditional horror novels, a best-selling, speculative thrillers series, a zombie young adult series, comics, movie novelizations, and nonfiction about horror, specifically the science and history behind the supernatural.

However, it is with *Ghost Road Blues,* the Bram Stoker Award–winning first novel in his classic, small-town horror Pine Deep Trilogy, that Maberry began his march toward horror master status.[3] *Ghost Road Blues* tells the story of the residents of Pine Deep, Pennsylvania, who thirty years ago killed a serial killer known as the Reaper. Since then, the town has seen peace and fame as the Halloween capital of America. But as the novel opens on the Halloween season, a new supernatural evil lurks on the outskirts of town, waiting to finish what the Reaper began.

Since *Ghost Road Blues,* Maberry has established a go-to style that readers can count on and seem to crave. His books all have chilling situations, menacing atmospheres, relentlessly fast-paced action, humor, and lots of gore. These are not books for the squeamish. Maberry liberally uses visual, aural, and scent-evoking adjectives that describe how the monsters, zombies, and humans (both heroes and villains) in his books fight for their lives.

Like Hill, Maberry makes use of flawed male protagonists. In Maberry's case most of the heroes come from troubled pasts, pasts in which they have erred and must now make things right. These heroes are in the thriller mode, meaning that their hearts are always in the right place despite their troubled pasts. They grapple with supremely evil villains, from supernatural monsters to terrorists. Maberry leaves no doubt as to who is on the side of justice in his books.

Maberry's books are also slightly faster paced than others in the genre. The action starts off fast and only increases. Besides using many fight scenes, Maberry employs multiple points of view, showing us the villain's plans, allowing readers to stay a step ahead of the hero, which increases both the pace and the reader's already heightened sense of dread. These high-stakes, intense cat-and-mouse games do lead to violent conclusions in which the hero triumphs, but the level of violence is not above and beyond what is typical to either the horror or thriller genre.

Previous to his success in the horror field, Maberry wrote extensively about martial arts, and, as a result, his characters tend to have martial arts backgrounds. Many readers enjoy this special bonus frame in his books.

Readers new to Jonathan Maberry should start with his Pine Deep trilogy, which begins with *Ghost Road Blues.*

Fans of Maberry may also enjoy Joe Hill, Brian Keene, and Gary Braunbeck because they all write character-centered horror with flawed but good-hearted protagonists. Like Maberry, Keene and Braunbeck create a mythology linking their novels. The influence of established horror writers like F. Paul Wilson, Richard Matheson, and Graham Masterton is reflected in Maberry's use of a menacing atmosphere and a speculative threat that is both evil and smart. The creepy thrillers of David Morrell will attract Maberry readers who love menacing atmospheres, fast-paced action, and plot twists galore, while the dark, supernatural adventure novels of James Rollins will draw Maberry readers who like the action-based plots, military details, and inclusion of scientific particulars.

THE OLD GUARD

Although Hill and Maberry have a death grip on their place at the top of the heap of the newer horror writers, there is a group that I will refer to as the Old Guard who have been scaring readers for the last thirty-plus years. And as they continue to publish relevant works, they are still attracting readers, new and old, in large numbers.

In this category, I place six writers who have demonstrated a sustained level of popularity that requires the attention of even the most horror-averse librarian: Stephen King, Peter Straub, Ramsey Campbell, Dean Koontz, F. Paul Wilson, and Dan Simmons. Their books are already lurking on your library shelves, being checked out multiple times a year, whether you know about them or not. Some of their work has strayed from the strict confines of horror literature, but they all continue to emphasize that menacing atmosphere which drew readers to their first horrific novels. Also, because these authors are read by a wide range of readers, many of whom would not consider themselves horror fans, it is important to understand their place in the world of genre fiction.

Stephen King

Stephen King should need no introduction. Forget horror; few writers have had more impact upon the entire literary community over the last thirty-five years than King. As a horror novelist, King has no peer. He has written in every major subgenre, mentored new authors, and brought dozens of his works to television and movie screens. In fact, most American readers today are introduced to horror through one of King's works. King also became an arbiter of popular culture, with a long-running column in the magazine *Entertainment Weekly,* where he spoke his mind on books, movies, music, and whatever else he felt like sharing. In early 2011, King put his column on hiatus, but during its run he moved many authors from obscurity to best-seller status with only a mention of their name.[4]

A typical King story line features fast-paced action and conversational language with misfit heroes tackling an evil that has been unleashed upon a normal world. King loves isolated settings, particularly the small towns of his native Maine, and he does not shy away from including sex and violence in his books. His fictional works are generally in the horror, psychological suspense, or dark fantasy genres. Recently, King's work has become popular with graphic novel illustrators, many of whom have worked with King to reproduce his compelling stories in a new format.

Although *The Stand* is King's best and most complete work, it is also over a thousand pages, making it a daunting starting point; therefore, I suggest readers new to King begin with *The Shining,* his classic and terrifying ghost story set in an isolated, haunted hotel.

Those who already enjoy King's work may also enjoy the horror of others profiled in this chapter, such as Joe Hill, Peter Straub, and Dean Koontz. The literary dark fantasy of Neil Gaiman is also a great choice as, like King, Gaiman uses the misfit hero to great effect. In the work of both storytellers, a loveable but hapless hero is begrudgingly called upon to stop an otherworldly threat. The adventure/suspense writing team of Douglas Preston and Lincoln Child is also a good choice for King fans. Their novels will appeal to the King fan who likes an action-based story written in colloquial language and in which a reluctant hero must overcome his personal limitations and demons before the evil force (be it human or monster) can be vanquished.

Peter Straub

Peter Straub is very similar to King; in fact the two have coauthored novels.[5] However, Straub's stories are a bit more dramatic and gruesome than King's. In terms of characters, Straub likes to center his stories on young, likable protagonists placed in difficult situations, such as having to share a dark secret. The difficulties increase, the mood darkens, and horrific consequences ensue. The world of a Straub novel is carefully constructed. He builds his books deliberately, continuously ratcheting up the fear and dread. Readers new to Straub should try *Ghost Story,* in which he begins with a suspicious death, leads into the nightmares of the survivors, throws in an isolated, snowed-in town setting, and finally introduces a zombie attack led by a female ghost out for revenge. See what I mean?

Fans of Straub should try Stephen King, but they may also enjoy the novels of Charles Grant in which the poor decisions of his characters lead to dark, paranormal consequences. John Saul's well-plotted tales, vivid details, and relentlessly escalating tension will also appeal to Straub fans. Finally, Robert McCammon is often forgotten when we talk about the Old Guard horror writers, but his consistently excellent novels, which blend history, mystery, suspense, and horror, would be a good match for Straub fans.

Ramsey Campbell

Widely considered Britain's greatest living horror writer, Ramsey Campbell is the third member of the Old Guard. He writes frightening, complex, and psychologically exhausting horror. Campbell often includes historical details and violent descriptions. But he is most noted for his relentless building of unease. Librarians should be aware that his heroes do not always emerge unscathed at the book's conclusion. Many a likable Campbell protagonist has been killed off. This feature could pose a problem for some traditional horror readers who expect the good guys to survive.

Readers new to Campbell should start with *Nazareth Hill,* an intense haunted house story in which a young girl is trapped in her home, pursued by an evil ghost, with no way out and no one to help her. For fans of Campbell who want to try something new, I would suggest Richard Laymon, Clive Barker, and Bryan Smith who also write intense and violent horror novels. For those who do not require an unearthly threat in their story but enjoy the extreme unease and the psychological intensity in Campbell's work, I would suggest Stephen Dobyns, whose novels, like Campbell's, make us question the evil within ourselves.

Intermission

Let's step back a moment before moving on to the last three members of the Old Guard. Although King, Straub, and Campbell write the majority of their books within the confines of the horror genre, the last three members, Koontz, Wilson, and Simmons, have begun to straddle the genre more. With roots that began in traditional horror, these three authors have explored other genre conventions in their works, so much so that many of their more recent novels may not be considered horror by the definition I have laid out. So why are they here? The answer is easy. Because many patrons still think of Koontz, Wilson, and Simmons as horror writers. Although narrow definitions of the genres aid us in our work, our readers' opinions trump all. Because readers have dubbed these authors horror masters, we still need to consider them in any discussion of the Old Guard.

Dean R. Koontz

It has been noted that Dean Koontz is the "least-known best-selling author in America."[6] Koontz is a fiercely private workaholic who writes eight to ten hours a day, every day, at his home. He does not actively promote any of his works, yet with every book, he sells millions of copies.

Koontz is not an author who fits neatly into a genre box. His work is more an amalgamation of the horror, thriller, science fiction, fantasy, and suspense genres. No matter into what genre you try to pigeonhole Koontz, his novels are marked by their menacing and nightmarish tones with story lines that pit good against evil. There are plenty of suspenseful plot twists in all Koontz's books. Violence and strong language also appear frequently, as do protagonists with supernatural abilities or powers that they do not completely understand.

Koontz's widely popular Odd Thomas paranormal series is a great example of both how Koontz writes and why fans love him.[7] Odd is a fry cook who can see and converse with dead people as well as identify evil spirits among us. Odd is an extremely likable character who uses his powers for good. The series is fast paced, suspense filled, and eerie. It is not pure horror, but it has many horror elements in a nightmare setting. Readers who had stopped reading Koontz over the years have come back to him in droves to follow Odd.

Although the Odd Thomas books are hugely popular right now, readers new to Koontz should go into his backlist and try *Watchers*, in which Travis Cornell has lost everyone: his parents, his wife, the members of his Special Forces squad. A trip to the mountains to clear his head instead begins an adventure involving super-intelligent animals, the National Security Agency, and contract killers.

Fans of Koontz should also try the horror novels of fellow Old Guard members F. Paul Wilson and Dan Simmons. John Saul is a great choice for Koontz readers who like the paranormal thrills and suspense of Koontz. Readers who do not require an unexplainable threat but really enjoy the dark, violent, and fast-paced suspense of Koontz might also enjoy John

Sandford and Jeffery Deaver. Fans specifically of Odd Thomas should not miss Jim Butcher's series following Harry Dresden.[8] Both Odd and Harry are reluctant paranormal investigators who must battle an evil lurking just under the surface of the "normal" world.

F. Paul Wilson

F. Paul Wilson is another of the Old Guard who, like Koontz, has made a career out of writing genre-blended novels. Wilson's books and stories regularly incorporate horror, science fiction, and thriller, but he unites it all with relentlessly paced, suspenseful story lines. These are the books of nightmares, set in gritty locales where supernatural evil is lurking behind every corner. The dark tone is lightened a bit by Wilson's strong, likable protagonists, who, like his popular series lead Repairman Jack, are intricately developed, original, and admirable. His secondary characters, including villains, also have a depth rarely seen among his genre peers.

Wilson has been around the block, writing traditional horror, horrific medical thrillers, and lots of short stories, but he has found his widest audience with his Repairman Jack novels. Jack has been described as a principled mercenary who lives off the grid in New York City. He has been engaged in an epic battle to keep an occult force at bay. With each new book in the series, Wilson has managed to keep Jack fresh, the stories original and suspenseful, and, most important, the fear palpable. *The Tomb* is the first book in the series.

Fans of Wilson would also enjoy the horror novels of Jonathan Maberry and fellow Old Guard member Dean Koontz, as well as the detailed characters, authentic settings, and intricately plotted situations of Robert McCammon. But without a doubt, fans of Repairman Jack who do not require a supernatural threat should turn to Lee Child and his more traditional suspense hero, Jack Reacher. Both series feature strong male heroes who live off the grid and get themselves tangled up in intricately plotted, high-suspense adventure.

Dan Simmons

The last of the Old Guard, Dan Simmons is also a genre-blending author, but with Simmons you can get any combination of horror, science fiction, suspense, thriller, and historical fiction. These are atmosphere-centered novels, with a deliberate pacing that allows the tension to build so intensely that it makes readers squirm. Simmons also develops complicated characters that we want to follow, even when we think we should know better. He includes interesting and thought-provoking details about real science or history or both in his books and then adds a twist of dark, otherworldly elements.

Recently, Simmons has added historical fiction to his genre-mix, so I would suggest readers new to Simmons begin with one of these titles, *The Terror*, which plays off the true story of the doomed Franklin expedition to find the Northwest Passage and supposes that a horrific and intelligent monster finally did them in.

Fans of Simmons should try these other authors who are known for their genre-defying literary thrillers with dark, supernatural twists: Ray Bradbury, Iain Banks, China Mieville, and Neal Stephenson.

THE PULP KINGS

Although the Old Guard authors began as more traditional horror writers and have expanded their reach over the years, a new brand of authors is carrying on the tradition of the good, old-fashioned horror story. And thank goodness too, because there are readers who crave these novels of zombies, monsters, witches, and the like. Librarians need to be familiar with these popular fearmongers.

I refer to these six authors—Brian Keene, Nate Kenyon, John Everson, Gary Braunbeck, Robert Dunbar, and Jeff Strand—as Pulp Kings because they write mainly paperback horror novels. They are the best of the newer generation of such writers; in fact, all the authors and titles included here are critically acclaimed if not award winners. Although each has his own style, all six authors rise above the mass of paperback horror offerings because of above-average character development and originality in storytelling. They also all use a fairly high level of gore in their stories, incorporate a large coming-of-age theme, and have their protagonists fighting villains both human and supernatural. Finally, it is important to note that these authors can be expected to release at least one novel a year and contribute to a few short story collections, all, quite possibly, for different publishers.

Brian Keene

Brian Keene tends to focus his award-winning stories on zombies and is considered a master at describing the dismemberment of bodies. Readers like Keene's wry sense of humor and his inclusion of popular culture references, as in *Castaways*, which is both an homage to the deceased horror legend Richard Laymon and a spoof of the reality TV show *Survivor*.[9] But anyone who has not yet read Keene should begin with *The Rising*, which started the current apocalyptic, zombie horror craze.

Nate Kenyon

Nate Kenyon is beginning to rise to the top of the genre with his compelling stories of psychologically scarred young people confronted by frightening evil. His characters are nuanced, the atmosphere tense, and the fear factor high. He has been consistently earning starred reviews in all the major library journals. Those new to Kenyon should try *Sparrow Rock*, in which a group of teenagers survives a nuclear blast in a bomb shelter only to realize that the outside world is full of mutant bugs that are turning humans into zombies.

■ ■ ■ ■ ■

The next three Pulp Kings share a major appeal: they all tend to set their stories in isolated settings, often coastal towns. They may change the monster who is stalking our heroes in each story, but each novel is oppressively claustrophobic. It is hard to escape when there is nowhere to go.

John Everson

John Everson likes to use newspaper reporters as his protagonists. He has them rooting around for a story and, in the process, finding more than they ever bargained for. He is also the bloodiest of the bunch and includes the most female characters, although they are quite often the villains. Everson's Bram Stoker Award–nominated *Covenant* is a great example of his work.[10] A reporter moves from the big city to a small coastal town only to stumble upon a string of mysterious teen suicides. In his attempt to investigate the story and save other young girls, he uncovers a huge secret that puts his own life and soul in mortal danger.

Gary Braunbeck

Gary Braunbeck and Robert Dunbar also produce the chills horror fans crave by creating a creepy small town and populating it with troubled protagonists, dark secrets, and evil, supernatural monsters. Braunbeck's setting of choice is Cedar Hill, Ohio. He writes smart, Midwest-flavored, gory stories in which readers are never quite sure whom they can trust, sometimes not until after the book is done. Talk about unsettling. If you have never read Braunbeck and want to experience the fear for yourself, start with *Coffin County*.

Robert Dunbar

Robert Dunbar sets his stories in dying towns filled with hopeless residents. The bleakness of the setting is only enhanced by the gruesome murders that begin taking place. Dunbar's monsters are usually related to folklore, in the ancient evil horror mode. For example, in *The Pines*, a town in the New Jersey Pine Barrens is under siege by a murdering force that may be connected to the mythological Jersey Devil. *The Pines* was originally published in 1989 and is still in print, which is a big feat for a paperback horror title. Dunbar may not have as many books as the other Pulp Kings, but he is still publishing and is extremely relevant. In fact in a 2009 review of his acclaimed story collection *Martyrs and Monsters, Dark Scribe Magazine* called Dunbar "the catalyst for the new literary movement in horror."[11] Dunbar is an author you need to know about.

Jeff Strand

The final Pulp King is Jeff Strand. For years Strand has been known for his witty and humorous horror novels, but recently he has moved into more serious horror with great success. In 2010, Strand released *Dweller*, an original, chilling, and heartbreaking work of horror fiction in which Toby, a young boy with no friends, retreats into the woods near his home to find peace. He also happens to find a monster living there—a monster named Owen, who becomes Toby's best friend for over fifty years. But when your best friend is an actual monster, he can inflict horrible things on your enemies. The novel has struck a chord with readers, and Strand is getting much more mainstream attention as a result.

■■■■■

Each of these authors can be used as a read-alike suggestion for the others. This is not to say that readers of one will like them all, but their tone, style, and overall themes are similar enough to offer as an option. They are quick reads, with engaging story lines, nightmarish atmospheres, and plenty of sex and gore. You can be assured that their quality is similar as each of these authors has been singled out by readers and their peers for awards. These are also the six paperback authors whom I would most recommend you purchase for inclusion in all general interest fiction collections.

Three more authors who could serve as read-alikes for Keene, Kenyon, Everson, Braunbeck, Dunbar, and Strand are Bryan Smith, Edward Lee, and Jack Ketchum. Smith, Lee, and Ketchum write extremely graphic horror novels in which the shock value often takes precedence over the storytelling. Although their work is popular, it may not fit in all general interest fiction collections. I suggest you familiarize yourself with their names and keep an eye on their releases to see if they will fit your readers' preferences and your collection development goals.

LADIES OF THE NIGHT

As is evident by the aforementioned authors, horror is still a very male-dominated world, but that does not mean there aren't good female writers producing top-notch horror, namely, Sarah Langan, Alexandra Sokoloff, Lisa Morton, Deborah LeBlanc, and Sarah Pinborough. What unites these women is more than their gender; they all are known for creating entertaining, terror-inducing novels, but with a lighter touch. The horror here is quiet. There can be gruesome scenes, but it is the creation of the unsettling atmosphere that rules the works of these women.

Sarah Langan and Alexandra Sokoloff

Sarah Langan and Alexandra Sokoloff are the most award-winning and the most widely read in the group. They are also great read-alikes for each other. Both focus on female protagonists encountering the supernatural. Langan specifically writes atmospheric works of horror and psychological suspense that lure the reader in with an engaging protagonist and thought-provoking situations. For example, in Langan's award-winning *The Missing*, a deserted town, which had previously been the site of an environmental disaster, is now releasing a virus that is turning people into thinking zombies.[12] This is a terrifyingly realistic and nightmarish novel.

The award-winning supernatural thriller and horror books by Alexandra Sokoloff are disturbingly creepy novels of paranormal activity that frighten without much gore. Sokoloff is known for creating a very detailed setting filled with dread—even when things appear to be going okay for the moment. She then lets her richly developed characters drive the action by having them face both their personal fears and the supernatural ones they encounter. Start reading Sokoloff with *The Harrowing*, in which a group of college students, who for varied reasons do not want to go home for the Thanksgiving holiday, unleash an evil spirit bent on wreaking havoc.[13]

It is important to note that from the first sentence, both Langan and Sokoloff set a dark and ominous tone that slowly builds throughout their engrossing novels, which culminate in a heart-racing final act. Fans of Langan and Sokoloff would also enjoy the quietly disturbing situations explored by Shirley Jackson in her novels and short fiction. Carol Goodman's psychological suspense, featuring female protagonists and set in isolated locations with hints of the supernatural, would also be a great read-alike option here.

Lisa Morton

Lisa Morton is an award-winning short-story writer and collection editor. Her work is consistently dark, unsettling, and frightening. In 2010 she released her first novel, *The Castle of Los Angeles,* and has proven that she will be a force to be reckoned with from now on. The "castle" of the title is a theater of which the female protagonist becomes the new owner. But something is not right. It is quiet horror, where subtle, disturbing things happen without any outright gory scenes. It is an introspective story, a ghost story, and a homage to the theater community, all in one. Fans of Sokoloff and Langan will love Morton.

Deborah LeBlanc

Deborah LeBlanc is an important figure in the horror community. She is the "anti-Sookie." Like Charlaine Harris's enormously popular paranormal Sookie Stackhouse series, LeBlanc's novels are set in the South, but unlike Harris's paranormal romances, there is nothing lovable about LeBlanc's nightmare world and the creatures that inhabit it. Readers who want their Southern horror full of atmosphere, blood, and nightmares could start with *A House Divided.* When a contractor literally tries to split an old Gothic mansion in two, he unleashes an evil force that is now out to destroy him.

Sarah Pinborough

Sarah Pinborough is the best-known British female horror writer. She writes horror novels and teleplays for fantasy and science fiction series on the BBC. Pinborough differs from her fellow Ladies of the Night in that she uses more fantasy elements in her horror novels. But like that of the other women, her horror is quiet, subtle, and absolutely terrifying. Readers new to Pinborough should start with *The Taken*, a chilling novel about a ghost out for revenge.

■■■■■

Two newer female writers in the field are Caitlin Kiernan and Sarah Jane Stratford. Both have stuck with horror for now but may move more into the paranormal genres. Only time will tell if they will earn a true place as Ladies of the Night. Interested readers should begin with Kiernan's *The Red Tree* and Stratford's *The Midnight Guardian*.

MOVING ON . . .

Today's tales of terror are varied. With a mix of the old guard and new voices, hardcover and paperback releases, and male and female faces to the fear, there is something for every reader at your library. The next nine chapters will delve even farther into the world of horror fiction, providing subgenre-based annotated lists of horror "sure bets" to offer to your patrons. The lists are focused on the current state of horror in the twenty-first century with a nod to the backlist gems that are already lurking on your shelves. These are proven winners that you can hand to your patrons with confidence. So gather your courage, and let's plunge farther into the darkness.

NOTES

1. Karen E. Taylor, "No More Silver Mirrors: The Monsters of Our Times," in *On Writing Horror: A Handbook by the Horror Writers Association*, rev. ed., ed. Mort Castle (Cincinnati, OH: Writer's Digest Books, 2006), 137.
2. *Heart-Shaped Box* won the 2007 Bram Stoker Award for best first novel.
3. *Ghost Road Blues* won the 2006 Bram Stoker Award for best first novel.
4. Stephen King, "The Pop of King," *Entertainment Weekly*, 1990–.
5. Stephen King and Peter Straub, *The Talisman* (New York: Random House, 2001), *The Black House* (New York: Random House, 2001).

6. Karen Springen as quoted in Joan G. Kotker, *Dean Koontz: A Critical Companion* (Westport, CT: Greenwood Press, 1996), 9.

7. Dean Koontz's Odd Thomas series begins with *Odd Thomas* (New York: Bantam Books, 2004).

8. Jim Butcher's Dresden Files series begins with *Storm Front* (New York: Roc Books, 2007).

9. In the introduction to *Castaways* (New York: Leisure Books, 2009), Keene explains how he based the de-evolved monsters in the novel on the work of Richard Laymon. Also, the characters are participants in a reality television show based on *Survivor* (distributed by Paramount Home Entertainment) except, in Keene's work, they must literally survive the monsters that are trying to kill them.

10. *Covenant* was nominated for the 2004 Bram Stoker Award for best first novel.

11. www.darkscribemagazine.com/reviews/martyrs-monsters-robert-dunbar.html (accessed October 7, 2010).

12. *The Missing* won the 2007 Bram Stoker Award for best novel.

13. *The Harrowing* was nominated for a 2007 Bram Stoker Award for best first novel. Interestingly, the other authors nominated in that year's category for best first novel are all mentioned in this chapter: Nate Kenyon, Sarah Langan, and the winner that year, Jonathan Maberry. That class of 2007 really has some staying power.

TITLE/AUTHOR LIST

Black House, by Stephen King and Peter Straub

The Castle of Los Angeles, by Lisa Morton

Coffin County, by Gary Braunbeck

Covenant, by John Everson

Dweller, by Jeff Strand

Ghost Road Blues, by Jonathan Maberry

Ghost Story, by Peter Straub

The Harrowing, by Alexandra Sokoloff

Heart-Shaped Box, by Joe Hill

Horns, by Joe Hill

A House Divided, by Deborah LeBlanc

Martyrs and Monsters, by Robert Dunbar

The Midnight Guardian, by Sarah Jane Stratford

The Missing, by Sarah Langan

Nazareth Hill, by Ramsey Campbell

The Pines, by Robert Dunbar

The Red Tree, by Caitlin Kiernan

The Rising, by Brian Keene

The Shining, by Stephen King

Sparrow Rock, by Nate Kenyon

The Stand, by Stephen King

The Taken, by Sarah Pinborough

The Talisman, by Stephen King and Peter Straub

The Terror, by Dan Simmons

The Tomb, by F. Paul Wilson

Watchers, by Dean R. Koontz

4

THE CLASSICS
Time-Tested Tales of Terror

In readers' advisory it is important to isolate "classic" titles for several reasons. First, some readers actively seek the best titles. Titles that have received continuous praise over a long period greatly appeal to these readers. Second, many patrons expect libraries to create core lists. It is one of our primary activities. Horror should not be left out here. Third, classics in any genre are a great introduction to the tropes and themes you will find throughout a genre. For these reasons, and doubtless others, including horror classics in your general interest collection, spending the time it takes to identify them, and reading some of them yourself will take you a long way toward better service to your horror readers.

Obviously the next step is to identify which horror titles should be considered classic examples of the genre, both to make sure you own them and to be able to articulate a core list for patrons.

To do this, start with a time limit. To be included on my list, each work must have been originally published before 1974. Why 1974? A book needs to be at least thirty years old to have earned the right to be considered a classic, but more important, 1974 was the year Stephen King published his first book, *Carrie*. Because the appearance of King and his enormous popularity marked a turning point in the genre, to be considered a "classic" a horror title must have first appeared before 1974. The genre changed so much after Stephen King entered the scene that you really need to consider pre-King titles in a category separate from post-King books.

In addition, these works must be easily available in most general public library collections. They need to still be in print so that replacement copies can be ordered. These need to be titles that you can get your hands on easily, both to look at yourself and to put in the appropriate readers' hands. Thankfully, many of these titles are already in the public domain and have received renewed interest with the proliferation of e-books. Once a title is in the public domain, e-book readers can download a copy for free, making these classic titles even more popular and accessible.

A list of classics is useless if it includes books that would not still be enjoyed by a twenty-first-century reader. The classics listed here are all well-written and engaging books that have proven their appeal to millions of readers. I have also included titles that are "good reads." Most readers' advisors keep a list of Best Bets or Good Reads around for the inevitable patron who, despite your prodding for more specific information, only wants you to find her "a good book." Many of the titles on this list sit in my Good Reads file, and they have yet to disappoint. So whether you are trying to find something different for a patron who feels stuck in a rut, need a book for a tried-and-true horror fan, or are just looking for a good read, you will find this list very helpful as you assist a wide range of patrons.

To ensure the list's authenticity, I consulted a number of authoritative sources to reflect a consensus. Those sources were an article by horror author Robert Weinberg titled "What You Are Meant to Know: Twenty-One Horror Classics"; *Hooked on Horror III: A Guide to Reading Interests* by Anthony J. Fonseca and June Michele Pulliam; Stephen Jones and Kim Newman's *Horror: The 100 Best Books;* and *Fiction Core Collection,* 16th ed.[1] The resulting titles were chosen for their historical significance, readability, and accessibility, a trifecta to which all core lists should aspire. Although you may find that this list leaves out a few of your personal favorites, it stands as a strong representation of the history of horror. These twenty influential books were chosen to highlight the history of the horror genre. This list is by no means the final word; rather, it should be seen as a conversation starter. As with all subgenre lists in this book, I will conclude the chapter with Becky's Picks of the top three titles.

Blatty, William Peter. *The Exorcist.*

The quintessential possession tale, *The Exorcist* is the novelization of a "true" story of the possession of a young girl in the 1940s. When 11-year-old Reagan is possessed by an ancient demon, a group of adults assembles to save her. This novel is still as raw and powerful as when it first came out. It is still the standard by which all demonic possession stories are judged.

Bradbury, Ray. *Something Wicked This Way Comes.*

When a carnival comes to a small Illinois town a week before Halloween, two adolescent boys are forever changed by its mysteries, secrets, and horrors. This novel begins tamely but ultimately packs a terrifying punch. Bradbury is a master of blending speculative genres into highly enjoyable and thought-provoking works. Here he presents a tense, tightly wound horror novel that will be sure to appeal to a wide range of readers.

Brontë, Emily. *Wuthering Heights.*

Driven mad by his thwarted love, Heathcliff seeks to destroy the Linton and Earnshaw families after the death of his beloved Catherine. Revenge, however, cannot calm the deluded Heathcliff, who is forever haunted by Catherine's ghost at Wuthering Heights. The novel is a great choice for fans of both traditional Gothic tales and ghost stories. Brontë's established place in the canon of Western classics also raises its profile. The horror here is both in the atmosphere and in the reader's sense of impending doom.

Doyle, Arthur Conan. *Tales of Terror and Mystery.*

This collection of Doyle's non-Holmes tales, most originally published in 1909, illustrates the famous mystery author's intense interest in the occult. The "terror" stories in this volume are fear-inducing creepfests filled with monsters, ghosts, and supernatural evil. These are not Sherlock Holmes whodunits, but rather satisfyingly frightful reads. Due to its public domain copyright status, this collection is seeing renewed interest in the e-book market. It will expose a new generation of readers to a different side of the classic author.

du Maurier, Daphne. *Rebecca.*

Mrs. de Winter may be a new bride, but she is not the first Mrs. de Winter; the deceased Rebecca previously held that honor. And though Rebecca is physically dead, she is still very much a force for the new Mrs. de Winter to contend with. In the last decade *Rebecca* has become a popular choice among book discussion groups.

Hawthorne, Nathaniel. *The House of the Seven Gables.*

The Pyncheons of Salem, Massachusetts, may be one of the most distinguished families in town, but they are also held victim to a centuries-old curse. Hawthorne based this novel on the curse a witch once placed on his own family. Current high interest in the history of witches will drive interest in Hawthorne's creepy classic.

Irving, Washington. *The Legend of Sleepy Hollow.*

In this classic story, love and a headless horseman collide. Our narrator, Ichabod Crane, a schoolteacher, moves to Sleepy Hollow, New York, where he falls in love with a local woman and is stalked by the ghost of a dead Revolutionary War soldier. Based on a German folktale, *The Legend of Sleepy Hollow* is an excellent example of a story with an unsettling atmosphere. Its inclusion on many high school American Lit reading lists, and the Tim Burton–directed movie starring Johnny Depp, also means your patrons will be familiar with this captivating story.

Jackson, Shirley. *The Haunting of Hill House*.

Often cited as the most terrifying haunted house story ever told, *The Haunting of Hill House* focuses on four strangers who come together for a stay in a notoriously haunted mansion. What transpires during their stay is both physically and emotionally terrifying. This is a novel that terrorizes the reader without actually depicting any gore. Jackson's brilliance and influence are receiving renewed recognition with modern readers. This, her most well-regarded novel, is a wonderful suggestion for readers who want psychological suspense, horror, or dark fantasy stories.

James, Henry. *The Turn of the Screw*.

Two small children on their uncle's estate are put in the care of a young governess. Everything is going well until the uncle's servant and the previous governess return from the dead to collect the souls of the children. This is a very subtle novel that leaves much unexplained, but this confusion enhances the fear. Today's readers will appreciate this complex and psychological tale.

James, M. R. *Casting the Runes and Other Ghost Stories*.

This single-volume collection of twenty-one of James's best stories, most of which were originally published in the early twentieth century, is a great introduction to horror's most influential ghost story writer. James's stories range from the blatantly supernatural to those which sit just over the edge of plausibility. With a new introduction by best-selling and Pulitzer Prize–winning author Michael Chabon, this collection of James's works stands out. Chabon's influence will help draw readers to this classic author.

Le Fanu, Joseph Sheridan. *Carmilla*.

Predating *Dracula* by twenty-five years, *Carmilla* is a Gothic story about the relationship between a female vampire, Carmilla, and her innocent friend, Laura. This is a surprisingly sexual novel in which Laura is both in love with Carmilla and repelled by her unnatural tendencies. *Carmilla* is a novel that will be enjoyed by all vampire fans, from those who prefer horror through readers of paranormal romance.

Levin, Ira. *Rosemary's Baby.*

In this chilling tale, a young woman gives birth to Satan's spawn. What makes this novel so terrifying is that although we know it is fiction, it feels like it could actually happen. A sequel, *Son of Rosemary,* follows the boy as an adult. With the critical acclaim for and the continued popularity of the movie version of *Rosemary's Baby,* readers frequently request this classic title.

Lovecraft, H. P. *The Dunwich Horror and Others.*

Mostly published in the years between World War I and World War II in the magazine *Weird Tales,* Lovecraft's stories have been collected in many volumes, and this one is simply a suggested starting point. Largely unknown during his lifetime, Lovecraft has become a cult figure in the horror community. His novelette-length stories, including "The Dunwich Horror," "The Thing on the Doorstep," and "The Call of Cthulhu," are the best places to begin. All Lovecraft stories feature monsters, possibly from another planet, wreaking havoc on the human world. Readers of supernatural fiction of all types will find something to love in Lovecraft.

March, William. *The Bad Seed.*

Amid the happy homes of suburbia, evil lurks in the form of a seemingly sweet and innocent young girl, Rhoda Penmark. Rhoda will kill if she does not get her way. What can her family do to stop the serial killer they have spawned? March is credited with creating the popular category of the "evil child" tale. The popular movie version of *The Bad Seed* as well as a recent publisher reissue including supplementary materials to encourage use for book discussion have raised this classic title's twenty-first-century profile.

Poe, Edgar Allan. "The Tell-Tale Heart."

Poe's stories continue to provide ample chills, even for twenty-first-century readers. They also continue to defy modern genre classification attempts, but horror readers will especially love the terrifying atmosphere Poe creates in "The Tell-Tale Heart." Here a man is driven crazy by his employer's eye, compelling the man to murder. After hiding the body in the floorboards, the murderer continues to hear the beating of the dead man's heart. "The Tell-Tale Heart" is included in most Poe collections.

Shelley, Mary. *Frankenstein.*

Often cited as the first horror novel ever written, *Frankenstein* is the story of a scientist's effort to create life. Shelley uses her Gothic novel to describe the horrors humankind can expect to confront when it foolishly tries to conquer nature. Although many modern readers will no longer find *Frankenstein* "scary," its place in the history of the genre cannot be denied. It is also a title that most of your patrons will be familiar with, even if they have never actually read it.

Stevenson, Robert Louis. *The Strange Case of Dr. Jekyll and Mr. Hyde.*
In nineteenth-century London, Dr. Jekyll performs an experiment in which he attempts to separate his pure, good side from his dark, evil qualities. He succeeds and splits his personality in two, but his other half is the evil Mr. Hyde. Stevenson's classic takes the speculative science that has become the popular starting point of twenty-first-century horror and combines it with a frightening psychological element that has stood up to the test of time.

Stoker, Bram. *Dracula.*
You may have heard of Dracula, but have you ever read the book? Count Dracula hides during the day, but from dusk to dawn he has the strength of twenty men, can summon armies of rats, and, oh yes, seeks human victims from whom he can suck their blood. Written in an epistolary style, *Dracula* is compelling, suspenseful, and surprising. You may need to keep multiple copies of this classic novel on the shelf. It continues to suck in new readers over 100 years after its first publication.

Walpole, Horace. *The Castle of Otranto.*
In this Gothic romance, Conrad, the heir to Otranto, is mysteriously ill. To keep the family dynasty intact, Conrad's father plans to take his son's place at the wedding altar—that is, until supernatural forces get in the way. *The Castle of Otranto* has been cited as introducing many of the tropes we still see in horror today, such as mysterious sounds, the opening of doors without human intervention, and the screaming, running woman being pursued by a "monster." This novel will appeal to fans of paranormal romance as well as those interested in classic horror.

Wells, H. G. *The Invisible Man.*
A stranger covered in bandages comes to the small English town of Iping. He has discovered the secret of making himself invisible, but soon finds this power makes his life much harder. After committing a murder, he becomes the victim of a manhunt. Wells's work has a very modern feel as it probes the saying, "Be careful what you wish for."

Current readers will find this cautionary tale has much in common with today's zombie stories.

BECKY'S CLASSICS PICKS

The Dunwich Horror, by H. P. Lovecraft

The Exorcist, by William Peter Blatty

The Haunting of Hill House, by Shirley Jackson

NOTE

1. Robert Weinberg, "What You Are Meant to Know: Twenty-One Horror Classics," in *On Writing Horror: A Handbook by the Horror Writers Association*, rev. ed., ed. Mort Castle (Cincinnati, OH: Writer's Digest Books, 2006); Anthony J. Fonseca and June Michele Pulliam, *Hooked on Horror III: A Guide to Reading Interests* (Westport, CT: Libraries Unlimited, 2009); Stephen Jones and Kim Newman, eds., *Horror: The 100 Best Books* (New York: Carroll and Graf, 1988); *Fiction Core Collection*, 16th ed. (New York: H. W. Wilson, 2010).

TITLE/AUTHOR LIST

The Bad Seed, by William March

Carmilla, by Joseph Sheridan Le Fanu

Casting the Runes and Other Ghost Stories, by M. R. James

The Castle of Otranto, by Horace Walpole

The Collected Tales of Edgar Allan Poe, by Edgar Allan Poe

Dracula, by Bram Stoker

The Dunwich Horror and Others, by H. P. Lovecraft

The Exorcist, by William Peter Blatty

Frankenstein; or, the Modern Prometheus: The 1818 Text, by Mary Shelley

The Haunting of Hill House, by Shirley Jackson

The House of the Seven Gables, by Nathaniel Hawthorne

The Invisible Man, by H. G. Wells

Rebecca, by Daphne du Maurier

Rip Van Winkle and Other Stories, by Washington Irving

Rosemary's Baby, by Ira Levin

Something Wicked This Way Comes, by Ray Bradbury

Son of Rosemary, by Ira Levin

The Strange Case of Dr. Jekyll and Mr. Hyde and Other Tales, by Robert Louis Stevenson

Tales of Terror and Mystery, by Arthur Conan Doyle

The Turn of the Screw and Other Stories, by Henry James

Wuthering Heights, by Emily Brontë

5

GHOSTS AND HAUNTED HOUSES
Home, Scream Home

Many a child has been introduced to the horror genre with a ghost story. Think back to your own childhood, for example: hearing ghost stories around the campfire, being told about the neighborhood haunted house, and, if you're a bit younger, reading the hugely popular Goosebumps books.[1] As we enter late childhood, we begin to understand that all things eventually die, including ourselves. We then spend the rest of our lives coming to terms with our own mortality. The ghost story, and its implicit message of life after death, is, in a sense, oddly comforting. We hear, read, and see films of ghost stories everywhere throughout our lives. The ghost story is probably the most common connection people have with horror fiction. So it should come as no surprise that ghosts and their haunting have emerged as one of the most pervasive and popular themes in the horror novel throughout history.

As mentioned in chapter 1, horror fiction as we know it today began with the Gothic ghost story, such as *The Castle of Otranto* (Walpole) and *Wuthering Heights* (E. Brontë), where creepy old mansions filled with dark secrets were commonly haunted by ghosts out for revenge. The ghost story evolved, and by the end of the nineteenth century, works like Henry James's *The Turn of the Screw* had become much more psychological in nature. The ghost began to reflect the inner feelings of the haunted party, his guilt, remorse, and paranoia. Throughout the late twentieth century and into the twenty-first, the ghost story has remained relevant and fresh. In fact, most of the major horror writers have tried their hand at the ghost story, and many have won awards for their efforts.

Although the ghost story has evolved over hundreds of years, there are basic characteristics that you and your readers can expect from all works within this subgenre. First, the main conflict that must be addressed and then resolved in every ghost story is why the spirit cannot rest. The author leads the reader into a situation where the protagonist is haunted by a ghost, a ghost that has its own reasons for roaming the living world. Our protagonist is suffering the consequences of being haunted, but until he or she can figure out why the ghost cannot rest in peace, the horror will continue. As a result, much of the plot of a ghost story revolves around an investigation of the ghost's living time on Earth, looking into why the spirit has returned from the dead and helping the ghost obtain what it needs to rest. The protagonist cannot defeat the spirit until this information is gathered and then used to quell the disembodied soul.

Second, the ghost sightings themselves are generally a reflection of the complex internal feelings of the person seeing the spirits. Guilt is the most common of these feelings. I do not mean to say that the ghost is merely a projection of the protagonist's inner turmoil. No, the ghosts in these stories are real, and the havoc they wreak is not a figment of anyone's imagination. But, in the ghost story, the characters that are being aggressively haunted always have dark secrets of their own, secrets they have avoided confronting. Through the course of the story the protagonists must fight the ghost and their own inner demons. Surviving their ordeal depends as much upon how the characters figure out the ghost's motivations as it does upon their own willingness to confront personal mistakes.

Finally, ghost stories play on the universal human fear of "things that go bump in the night." This subgenre is dominated by dark corners, old creaky houses, terrible tragedies, and untimely deaths. The specters that appear when the lights go out are not for the faint of heart. Humans may have conquered the dark thousands of years ago, but ever since that first spark of fire illuminated the night, we have remained frightened of the shadows. The ghost story (like vampire and werewolf tales) is dependent upon darkness; the hauntings most often occur where lights are dim, so that the haunted can never be absolutely sure of what they just witnessed.

Ghost stories appeal to readers for many reasons. First, they affirm a belief in life after death. Although most of us do not want to be forced to roam the halls of someone else's home for the rest of eternity, reading about these lingering spirits reassures us that something happens to our spirit after our body ceases to live. It is less frightening to think about living in a haunted house than it is to confront our own mortality. Second, readers enjoy ghost stories for the psychological element involved in working out both the spirit's motivations and the protagonist's dark secrets. Third, ghost stories have a reliable pacing that begins eerily measured and methodically builds to a dramatic climax filled with action and surprises. Finally, the ghost story's setting, generally a creepy old house, is a big draw for readers. The nooks, the creaks, and the hidden secrets are favorites of ghost story fans.

Because these works appeal to some of our basic human fears, are fueled by compelling internal conflicts, and have been a part of our story-telling tradition from childhood on, it should come as no surprise that the novels in this subgenre cover a wide range of subjects. There is a ghost story tailored to just about every reader. For those who enjoy romance there are numerous works by Barbara Erskine and Barbara Michaels.[2] If it is a detective story your readers crave, they could try *Haunted* (Herbert) or *A Room for the Dead* (Hynd). There are even ghost tales with elements of science fiction and fantasy like *The House on the Borderland* (Hodgson).

The titles that follow focus on the present state of the ghost story, with a few well-placed nods to the past. These sure-bet tales of ghosts and haunted houses offer readers entrance to a world where haunting is the norm.

Agarwal, Shilpa. *Haunting Bombay.*

Agarwal's debut novel set in 1960s Bombay is an example of the power of the ghost story throughout the world. Teenager Pinky unbolts a door in the family home, unleashing the ghost of a baby and her midwife. The ghosts' appearances throw the entire family into chaos as they have to battle the apparitions and their own family secrets. *Haunting Bombay* is of the subtle and atmospheric horror mold like the stories by Alexandra Sokoloff or Sarah Langan. Its setting also takes advantage of the current popularity of fiction set in India.

Bear, Greg. *Dead Lines.*

Award-winning science fiction writer Greg Bear presents a terrifying story of a new technology opening a path to another dimension. The dead have been not so happily woken, and what appeared to be a super-fast new communication device may be killing its users. This is a high-tech, fast-paced ghost story in which the atmosphere and fear greatly exceed the scientific detail. *Dead Lines* is a chilling thrill ride of twenty-first-century horror.

Campbell, Ramsey. *Nazareth Hill.*

As a young child, Amy sees a ghost through the window of Nazarill, a run-down building. Eight years later, after Amy's father becomes the caretaker of the now renovated building, an older tenant dies. Before it is too late, Amy must convince everyone that his death is the work of a ghost out for revenge. Campbell has more recent titles, but this one is still among his most terrifying.

Clegg, Douglas. *Mischief.*

The magnificent Harrow House, which has been empty for decades because of the terrible things that happened there, is restored and reopened as a boys' boarding school. The boys embrace the mythology of the mansion's ghosts, but little do they know the true terror that awaits them. Clegg is a master at harnessing the reader's fear and injecting it right into the story. This is one ghost story you may have to read with the lights on.

Datlow, Ellen, and Nick Mamatas, eds. *Haunted Legends.*

Gathered by Datlow, the best-known editor in the world of horror, *Haunted Legends* is a spooky collection of ghost stories in the classic style written by some of the biggest names in contemporary horror. This standout combination of traditional storytelling, Datlow's award-winning editing, and a modern sensibility will be sure to appeal to a wide range of readers.

Farris, John. *Phantom Nights.*

It is a hot August night in rural Tennessee in 1952 when a mute teenager, Alex, witnesses the rape and murder of a female nurse by U.S. Senate candidate Leland Howard. Leland's influence seems to be enough for him to get away with his crime, but Alex has a secret: he can communicate with the dead woman's ghost. What follows is an original, supernatural crime story with compelling characters, a well-developed setting, and plenty of ghosts out for revenge.

Garton, Ray. *The Loveliest Dead.*

In this despair-filled story of a full-scale, terrifying haunting, a young couple and their surviving son relocate after the death of the couple's 4-year-old son. What is supposed to be a fresh start becomes a nightmare as the family's backyard is infested with very ugly, child ghosts, one of whom looks just like the couple's dead son. This is a slowly building tale that draws you in, grabs you, and propels you to the finish headfirst.

Gout, Leopoldo. *Ghost Radio.*

Joaquin is the host of a popular paranormal call-in show in Mexico. As he prepares to take the show to an American audience, the ghosts of the past are literally stalking him. When Joaquin has had enough, he decides to confront the ghosts who are slowly driving him mad; however, that choice may be the key to his ultimate undoing. This story is creepy and unsettling. Gout puts the reader directly into Joaquin's confused head to heighten the tension. *Ghost Radio* also has wonderful illustrations.

Hill, Joe. *Heart-Shaped Box.*

Jude Coyne is an aging rock star, obsessed with the supernatural. On an Internet auction site, he buys an old suit that is said to come with a ghost. Thinking the story a joke, Coyne buys the suit and ends up getting much more than he bargained for. The ghost has a personal vendetta against Coyne, and the two spend the novel in a struggle over Coyne's past mistakes and, ultimately, his life. This is a title by the best young horror writer today, and it is destined to become a classic.

Keene, Brian. *Dark Hollow.*

In this fast-paced story of a haunted wood, Adam, a writer, is having marital problems. While walking through the woods near his home, Adam comes upon a woman in a sexual situation with a statue. As more women begin disappearing into the woods, the men are forced to confront the spirit responsible. This is a steamy novel filled with danger, dark places, and legends. Keene returns to the action of *Dark Hollow* in *Ghost Walk*.

King, Stephen. *The Shining.*

Jack Torrance brings his family along on his new job as the winter caretaker of the Overlook Hotel in the isolated Colorado mountains. In true King fashion, we find that this is not your ordinary hotel, as it is haunted by spirits that are trying to take over the family. *The Shining* is both the standard-bearer of the modern ghost story and one of King's best novels. *The Tommyknockers* and *Bag of Bones* are also solid King ghost stories.

Langan, Sarah. *The Keeper.*

Bedford, Maine, is a small, down-on-its-luck town, haunted by the ghost of Susan Marley. Susan's troubled past and violent death initiate a series of events that leave the entire town reeling. The dead rise from their graves, townsfolk are gripped with homicidal thoughts, and everyone is fighting to simply survive. This award winner has a wide appeal.

LeBlanc, Deborah. *A House Divided.*

In this lush, character-centered, Southern ghost story, LeBlanc follows a greedy contractor as he buys an old home and literally splits it in two during its renovation. His actions release a terrifying ghost, out to destroy he who awakened it.

Masterton, Graham. *House of Bones.*

The prolific Masterton centers this haunted house story around a real estate agency run by the creepy Mr. Vane. When John begins working at the agency, he visits one of Vane's special listings and accidentally discovers a horrible secret about the property: something inside it is brutally killing people. As victims pile up, John investigates and becomes pursued himself. Can John survive working for Vane and the spirits he controls? *House of Bones* is a fast-paced, suspenseful, and terrifyingly believable ride by a consistently good horror writer.

Pinborough, Sarah. *The Taken.*

Thirty years after her death, 13-year-old sociopath Melanie Parr has come back as a ghost to exact revenge thanks to a spirit called the Catcher Man, who is able to hold children in a state between life and death. This British horror novel is terrifying without gore and has a well-described setting as well as a sympathetic but reluctant protagonist.

Saul, John. *Nathaniel.*

Horror master Saul's best ghost story is one of his earliest novels. When her husband, Mark, dies, Janet and her son Michael return to Mark's hometown for the funeral. There Janet finds a farm she never knew Mark owned, and Michael discovers the town's secret, a boy named Nathaniel who has haunted the community for over a century. *The Blackstone Chronicles,* a serialized ghost story, is also a strong standout in this subgenre.

Simmons, Dan. *A Winter Haunting.*

"Forty-one years after I died, my friend Dale returned to the farm where I was murdered," begins Simmons's terrifying look into ghosts and madness. Although with *A Winter Haunting,* Simmons returns to the characters of 1991's *Summer of Night,* this novel stands on its own as an engrossing fright fest with nods to the classics in the haunted house subgenre. For a look into a haunted city, also try *Song of Kali.*

Smith, Bryan. *House of Blood.*

While driving through the mountains in Tennessee, a group of young vacationers seeks refuge in an isolated, rundown house. However, this is no ordinary building. It is actually the portal to an underworld of spirits who are trying to return to the surface. Smith returns to the action with a bloody sequel, *Queen of Blood.*

Sokoloff, Alexandra. *The Unseen.*

In the 1960s, researchers and students from the Duke University Parapsychology Lab went to study poltergeists in a haunted house. No one returned unscathed. Today, Professor Laurel MacDonald and three others return to the haunted home in the hope of getting some answers, but are they prepared for what they will find? Also try *The Harrowing.*

Straub, Peter. *Ghost Story.*

After an elderly man dies, strange things start happening in the small town of Millburn, New York. The events force the deceased man's friends to come face-to-face with both a tragic event from their past and the ghosts currently marching upon their snowbound town. After decades of excellent, award-winning horror novels from Straub, this backlist title is still the place for readers new to Straub to start discovering him. For a newer ghost story by Straub, try *In the Night Room.*

BECKY'S GHOSTS AND HAUNTED HOUSES PICKS

Heart-Shaped Box by Joe Hill

Nazareth Hill by Ramsey Campbell

The Unseen by Alexandra Sokoloff

NOTES

1. R. L. Stine writes the Goosebumps series (New York: Scholastic).
2. In the first edition of this text, I suggested Barbara Erskine's *House of Echoes* (New York: Signet, 1997) and Barbara Michaels's *House of Many Shadows* (New York: Berkley, 1996).

TITLE/AUTHOR LIST

Bag of Bones, by Stephen King

The Blackstone Chronicles, by John Saul

Dark Hollow, by Brian Keene

Dead Lines, by Greg Bear

Ghost Radio, by Leopoldo Gout

Ghost Story, by Peter Straub

Ghost Walk, by Brian Keene

The Harrowing, by Alexandra Sokoloff

Haunted, by James Herbert

Haunted Legends, by Ellen Datlow and Nick Mamatas

Haunting Bombay, by Shilpa Agarwal

Heart-Shaped Box, by Joe Hill

A House Divided, by Deborah LeBlanc

House of Blood, by Bryan Smith

House of Bones, by Graham Masterton

The House on the Borderland, by William Hope Hodgson

In the Night Room, by Peter Straub

The Keeper, by Sarah Langan

The Loveliest Dead, by Ray Garton

Mischief, by Douglas Clegg

Nathaniel, by John Saul

Nazareth Hill, by Ramsey Campbell

Phantom Nights, by John Farris

Queen of Blood, by Bryan Smith

A Room for the Dead, by Noel Hynd

The Shining, by Stephen King

Song of Kali, by Dan Simmons

Summer of Night, by Dan Simmons

The Taken, by Sarah Pinborough

The Tommyknockers, by Stephen King

The Unseen, by Alexandra Sokoloff

Winter Haunting, by Dan Simmons

6

VAMPIRES
Books with Bite

Vampires are everywhere these days, but the vampires of today's popular culture are not all stalking their victims in the horror genre. In fact, the vampires of today's fiction bear little resemblance to the frightful, blood-sucking creatures found in history and folklore. In early tales of vampirism, individuals who were already of shady character or had been killed violently were seen as being more likely to return from the dead to feed on the living. Unlike the romanticized portrayals of vampires, which began with *Dracula* (Stoker) and reached a tipping point with *Interview with the Vampire* (Rice), these original vampires were hideous, partially decayed creatures that attacked living relatives and neighbors rather than beautiful aristocratic damsels in distress. The best film depiction of this type of vampire can be seen in the silent film *Nosferatu*.[1] Here the vampire is more animal than human, with grotesque fangs, pointy ears, and menacing fingernails. There is no trace of the sexy Edward Cullen here.[2]

Of course the most popular vampire ever is Dracula. First published by Bram Stoker in 1897, *Dracula* has never been out of print and has been translated into every major language in the world. Its intimate, epistolary style draws readers into the thoughts of the major players in the story. When people all over the world think of vampires, it is Dracula who first comes to mind. This novel provides a compelling, suspenseful, and frightening reading experience regardless of the time and place in which it is read.

Stoker's vampire was a handsome aristocrat. Women were drawn to him, yet when they succumbed to his charms, terror and mayhem ensued. This conflict has since been present in all vampire literature. The fear comes from both the power of the vampires and our sensual interest in them. For almost eighty years, vampires did not stray much from the

Dracula mold, and then Anne Rice released *Interview with the Vampire* in 1976. Rice's protagonist, the vampire Louis de Pointe du Lac, makes a confession to the reader. In the novel he recounts how he became a vampire, but, more interesting, he also expresses his torment and guilt over his situation. This approach is significant because it marks the beginning of the current trend in vampire literature: the reluctant and vulnerable vampire. This vampire wants to be human again, wants to be accepted by humans, and, as this new vampire is explored by other authors, wants to be loved.

Over the last thirty-five years, the issues first explored by Rice have evolved. As a result we now have two different vampire trajectories in fiction: the sympathetic (and quite possibly sexy) vampire versus the monster. Horror readers will be more drawn to the monster vampire stories, but librarians need to understand the trends. Just because a book has a vampire does not mean a horror reader will enjoy it. Thankfully for horror fans, many writers and readers have gotten bored with seeing only sexy vampires in print, and we are in the midst of a revival of the bloody, scary, and evil vampire. It is the monster trajectory that this chapter focuses on.

The following vampire books are horror books first and vampire books second. These vampire books all provoke terror with an uneasy atmosphere above all else. These are the vampires of your nightmares, not the ones with which you want to share your bed. I also have included annotations for the books in Rice's Vampire Chronicles series. Her novels may represent the beginning of a shift in the direction of the vampire story, but they also still satisfy many true horror readers. Because these are novels that are constantly checked out of the library, readers' advisors need to know about them.

Interestingly, there is no definitive list of the characteristics of the vampires you will find in these books. Vampires in literature are as varied as the prolific imaginations that created them. He or she may have fangs, but not always; light may be fatal, but some vampires can walk in the daylight; some kill their mortal meal while feeding, while others just stun their victims; some pass the vampirism on to their quarry, others simply enjoy a meal; some are disgusted by their need to drink blood and struggle against their cursed immortality, while others see themselves as a more advanced species, higher on the food chain than mere humans. The only constant in all vampire lore is the blood connection—the need to drink mortal blood (animal or human) to maintain a vampire's life.

Because this chapter focuses on the monster vampire rather than the romantic lead, popular series that feature vampires, such as the Sookie Stackhouse series (Harris), the Anita Blake, Vampire Hunter series

(Hamilton), or the Undead novels (Davidson), which do not actively try to evoke terror as their main appeal will not be included here.[3] For more help with your vampire-loving patrons, consult *Fang-tastic Fiction: Twenty-First Century Paranormal Reads* (ALA Editions, 2010), by Patricia O'Brien Mathews. In this resource you can find many lists of books for patrons looking for paranormal rather than horror stories. This chapter will also not discuss those series that feature vampires but put the pacing and investigative elements at the forefront of the story. These books, which include the popular Joe Pitt Casebook series (Huston) and the Strain Trilogy (de Toro), are classified as supernatural thrillers and are covered in chapter 13, "Moving beyond the Haunted House: Whole Collection Options for Horror Readers."[4]

Clark, Simon. *Vampyrrhic.*

Dr. David Leppington returns to the small British town that bears his family's name to see his dying uncle. The uncle lets David in on the town's big secret: there are vampires who rule the tunnels under the town. Soon David and his new friends are placed in the middle of a battle between the dead and the living, a battle that could threaten the entire world. This is a chilling but violent story. Clark revisits the world of *Vampyrrhic* in *Whitby Vampyrrhic.*

Cronin, Justin. *The Passage.*

A virus that turns people into vampires has decimated North America. Fed up with living in fear, a band of survivors joins a mysteriously ageless young girl and attempts to regain control of the world. *The Passage* is an absorbing, frightening, action-packed story that ends with the mother of all cliff hangers and a promise of two more installments. This novel was widely acclaimed as one of the best novels of 2010 in all fiction.

Garton, Ray. *Live Girls.*

Davey's life is not going well. He has lost his job and his girlfriend. His sister-in-law and niece have been murdered, and his brother is the main suspect. As he investigates the murder, he learns about a club called Live Girls. Although there are sexy women and plenty of temptations, there are also violent, demonic vampires who live in the club's basement. This is a fast-paced, violent, and sexually explicit tale of terror.

Grahame-Smith, Seth. *Abraham Lincoln: Vampire Hunter.*

With a bit of tongue-in-cheek humor, Grahame-Smith imagines that Abraham Lincoln, after witnessing his mother's death at the hands of a vampire, vows to spend his life as a vampire hunter. Using fabricated journals of our sixteenth president as a guide, this novel shows how Lincoln linked the evils of slavery and vampirism in his fight to save the Union. This book is mostly fun, with some frightening scenes, while the conversational style makes it extremely accessible.

Kent, Jasper. *Twelve.*

In this promising beginning to a projected historical horror series, Kent uses Napoleon's invasion of Russia as his backdrop. Russian troops call on a group of twelve men from a southern tribe to hold Napoleon back, but this tribe is unusually bloodthirsty. The Russian army soon loses control as the vampires ravage enemy and countrymen alike. These are scary and evil vampires who have been given free reign over a battered landscape.

King, Stephen. *'Salem's Lot.*

The streets of a small Maine town are empty by day because the citizens of Jerusalem's Lot have all become vampires. This novel is both horror and social commentary on the problems within insular communities in America. King's novel is a must-read for any vampire horror fan.

Kostova, Elizabeth. *The Historian.*

In this creepy literary thriller, a young woman begins researching the provenance of a mysterious book she finds among her father's belongings. The book has an ominous note and a chilling history linking it to Vlad the Impaler. As the protagonist dives further into her research, the story shifts among three time periods, the atmosphere gets more and more oppressive, and the bloodthirsty threat becomes terrifyingly real.

Laymon, Richard. *The Traveling Vampire Show.*

Normally known for his action-fueled plots, Laymon steps back a bit here and focuses on the atmosphere and characters of this vampire story. Dread builds deliberately as three teenagers sneak into an adults-only vampire show. Although there only to catch a glimpse of a real-life vampire, the teens end up in a fight for their lives. The action builds to a final battle scene that many say is the best ending to a horror novel . . . ever.

Lee, Edward. *Brides of the Impaler.*

A couple moves into their dream home only to find a secret evil in their basement, and this evil is guarded by a nun and her minions, a bunch of gibberish-speaking homeless women. As the title hints, this tale is Dracula inspired but with a modern twist. It is chilling and cinematic with a generous dollop of sex and violence.

Lindqvist, John Ajvide. *Let Me In.*
The title of this unique, dark take on the vampire tale, originally translated from the Swedish as *Let the Right One In,* was changed to reflect the title of the popular film adaptation in 2010. Twelve-year-old Oskar is a total outcast and obsessed with serial killers. Eli is a young, pale, foul-smelling girl who happens to also be a vampire. The two develop a macabre friendship that leads to violence as Eli tries to protect Oskar from being drowned by a gang of bullies. This is a haunting tale that will stay with you long after you finish it.

Marks, John. *Fangland.*
A young television producer is sent to Transylvania to interview a Romanian crime boss. As you can see, *Fangland* is deeply rooted in Stoker's *Dracula,* but while Marks loosely follows the classic's plot and style, *Fangland* is a frightening, bloody, and unsettling journey in its own right. This is Dracula for the twenty-first century's media-obsessed reader, with a larger amount of gore than Stoker could have ever imagined.

Masterton, Graham. *Descendant.*
During World War II, James Falcon was an American vampire hunter. Now in the late 1950s, James is recalled to fight an old enemy who has come back. This is a bloody and frightening vampire tale in which James must confront some of the scariest things from his past as well as battle an evil vampire. The unsettling story explores the characteristics of the vampires as well as the price of war. Readers could also try *Manitou Blood.*

Penzler, Otto, ed. *The Vampire Archives: The Most Complete Volume of Vampire Tales Ever Published.*
Throw out all your other vampire anthologies; this is the ultimate collection. Acclaimed editor Penzler has compiled over eighty stories and poems and grouped them in such categories as "Pre-Dracula," "Psychic Vampires," and "This Is War" to provide a snapshot of the vampire through time. Most important, the focus here is on horror. Add a preface by Neil Gaiman and a foreword by Kim Newman, and you have the collection that is a horror fan's dreams.

Rice, Anne. The Vampire Chronicles (in series order).

Interview with the Vampire

In an interview with a boy reporter, eighteenth-century plantation owner Louis de Pointe du Lac confesses how he came to be a vampire and his consequent torment and guilt.

The Vampire Lestat

Lestat, having risen after fifty years, awakens in the 1980s to the wonders of the modern world. He becomes a rock star and breaks centuries of self-imposed vampire silence by penning an autobiography of his childhood in eighteenth-century France, detailing how he came to be a vampire.

The Queen of the Damned

Akasha, Queen of the Damned, awakens after 6,000 years of sleep. Once the Queen of the Nile, Akasha is now intent on saving mankind from itself. Then there is Lestat, whose successful singing career has angered hundreds of other vampires. Throw in the twins Maharet and Mekare, who are haunting dreams the world over, and you have the ingredients for an all-out vampire showdown.

The Tale of the Body Thief

Lonely and full of doubts, Lestat makes a deal with Raglan James, a Body Thief who can switch souls with another being and who also happens to be a very talented con artist. Against the advice of his friends, Lestat agrees to temporarily switch bodies with the man, so that he can once again experience being mortal.

Memnoch the Devil

Lestat searches for Dora, a mortal with whom he has become infatuated, at the same time he is being stalked by a shadowy figure who turns out to be Memnoch, the Devil. Memnoch presents Lestat with unimagined opportunities: to witness creation and to visit purgatory. Lestat must ponder the ultimate question of what he believes to be good and evil.

The Vampire Armand

In fifteenth-century Constantinople, Armand recounts his memories of his childhood abduction from Kiev, how he was sold to Venetian artist and vampire Marius, how he was transformed into a vampire, and the subsequent love affair he had with his mentor.

Merrick

The vampires Lestat and Louis and the dead vampire child Claudia are introduced to the Mayfair Witches. Louis's obsession with raising Claudia's ghost to make amends elicits Merrick Mayfair's help.

Blood and Gold

Marius, the mentor of Lestat, the creator of Armand, and the lover of Pandora, tells of his 2,000-year existence and how he became the burdened protector of Akasha and Enkil, the parents of the very first vampires.

Blackwood Farm

A new, young vampire, Quinn Blackwood, seeks the help of Lestat to save his family. A doppelganger named Goblin is living with Quinn on his family's estate, and Goblin's power is strengthening out of control.

Blood Canticle

Lestat is back as the narrator for the first time since *Memnoch the Devil*, except now he wants to become a saint, an unrealistic option for vampires. He also helps Quinn make his true love, a witch, immortal. This account is a satisfying conclusion to the ten-volume series, with Rice bringing back many popular characters but easily connecting the dots for newer readers.

Stoker, Dacre, with Ian Holt. *Dracula: The Un-Dead.*

In this, the first ever authorized sequel to the original *Dracula,* we pick up the action twenty-five years later. Our heroes are much worse for the wear. Mina and Jonathan cannot find happiness together, as their son is a constant reminder of their terror, and death seems to always be near. Bram Stoker himself is even a character. This is a complex story that contemplates the nature of evil while providing a compelling read.

Stratford, Sarah Jane. *The Midnight Guardian.*

A group of 1,000-year-old vampires are on the loose in 1939 Nazi Germany. These "Millennials," as the vampires refer to themselves, do not want the Nazis to start a war, thus killing off their food supply. Stratford sets up her vampires and their mythology well. Although the Millennials are on the right side of history, that position does not mean they should be counted among the mortals' friends. This novel is reminiscent of the vampire classic *The Keep* (Wilson).

Strieber, Whitley. *The Last Vampire.*

In 1981, Strieber wrote *The Hunger,* one of the most original vampire novels. In it, he supposed that vampires created the human race and cultivated its civilization in order to ensure a food source. Twenty years later he revisited this world, only now the entire race of vampires is in danger. Can the 3,000-year-old vampire Miriam hold off a CIA vampire slayer and save her people? Strieber continues the series with *Lilith's Dream.*

Taylor, Terence. *Bite Marks: A Vampire Testament.*

In this urban fiction meets horror story, a young prostitute is killed by a vampire, brought back to life, and forced to feed on her baby. The young woman dies, but her now vampire baby escapes, jeopardizing all that has kept the vampires secret for centuries. This is a gritty and thrilling story with truly frightening moments. Watch as the vampires do whatever it takes to protect their race.

Wellington, David. *13 Bullets: A Vampire Tale.*

Featuring Wellington's signature style of high-octane action, bloody battles, and a plot that pits average people against violently evil supernatural beings, *13 Bullets* marks the start of his popular Vampire Tales series. In this first installment, a police patrol woman comes upon three vampires who have survived twenty years after their entire clan was destroyed. Once uncovered, the vampires are intent on both rebuilding their clan and exacting bloody revenge. The series is a modern take on the traditional vampire story, featuring FBI vampire hunters battling true evil. As the series progresses, a major plot twist ratchets up the terror factor exponentially. The story continues in *99 Coffins: A Historical Vampire Tale, Vampire Zero: A Gruesome Vampire Tale,* and *23 Hours: A Vengeful Vampire Tale.*

Wilson, F. Paul. *Midnight Mass.*

Horror master Wilson imagines a post–cold war world where vampires are taking over the planet. They have now reached America, and a motley crew of heroes including a nun, a priest, and a rabbi are trying to stop them. Particularly unsettling are the human "cowboys" who work for the vampires, rounding up humans in exchange for immortality. And don't forget Wilson's classic novel featuring vampires and Nazis, *The Keep.*

BECKY'S VAMPIRE PICKS

Let Me In, by John Ajvide Lindqvist

The Passage, by Justin Cronin

The Vampire Archives, edited by Otto Penzler

NOTES

1. *Nosferatu,* directed by F. W. Murnau (1922; New York: Kino International, 2007), 2 videodiscs.
2. Edward Cullen is the vampire love interest in Stephenie Meyer's popular series beginning with *Twilight* (New York: Little, Brown, 2005).
3. Charlaine Harris's Sookie Stackhouse novels begin with *Dead until Dark* (New York: Ace Books, 2001); Laurell K. Hamilton's Anita Blake, Vampire Hunter series begins with *Guilty Pleasures* (New York: Ace Books, 1993); MaryJanice Davidson's Undead novels begin with *Undead and Unwed* (New York: Berkley Sensation, 2004).
4. Charlie Huston's Joe Pitt Casebook series begins with *Already Dead* (New York: Ballantine, 2005); Guillermo de Toro's Strain Trilogy begins with *The Strain* (New York: William Morrow, 2009).

TITLE/AUTHOR LIST

13 Bullets: A Vampire Tale, by David Wellington

23 Hours: A Vengeful Vampire Tale, by David Wellington

99 Coffins: A Historical Vampire Tale, by David Wellington

Abraham Lincoln: Vampire Hunter, by Seth Grahame-Smith

Bite Marks: A Vampire Testament, by Terence Taylor

Blackwood Farm, by Anne Rice

Blood and Gold, by Anne Rice

Blood Canticle, by Anne Rice

Brides of the Impaler, by Edward Lee

Descendant, by Graham Masterton

Dracula: The Un-Dead, by Dacre Stoker and Ian Holt

Fangland, by John Marks

The Historian, by Elizabeth Kostova

The Hunger, by Whitley Strieber

Interview with the Vampire, by Anne Rice

The Keep, by F. Paul Wilson

The Last Vampire, by Whitley Strieber

Let Me In, by John Ajvide Lindqvist

Lilith's Dream, by Whitley Strieber

Live Girls, by Ray Garton

Manitou Blood, by Graham Masterton

Memnoch the Devil, by Anne Rice

Merrick, by Anne Rice

The Midnight Guardian, by Sarah Jane Stratford

Midnight Mass, by F. Paul Wilson

The Passage, by Justin Cronin

The Queen of the Damned, by Anne Rice

'Salem's Lot, by Stephen King

The Tale of the Body Thief, by Anne Rice

The Traveling Vampire Show, by Richard Laymon

Twelve, by Jasper Kent

The Vampire Archives: The Most Complete Volume of Vampire Tales Ever Published, edited by Otto Penzler

The Vampire Armand, by Anne Rice

The Vampire Lestat, by Anne Rice

Vampire Zero: A Gruesome Vampire Tale, by David Wellington

Vampyrrhic, by Simon Clark

Whitby Vampyrrhic, by Simon Clark

7

ZOMBIES
Follow the Walking Dead

Zombies are undead beings who become reanimated and begin wreaking havoc on the living. Their undead qualities are reminiscent of vampire legends, while their reanimation invariably recalls Shelley's *Frankenstein.* The earliest known zombie tales were set in the West Indies and involved the creature being revived by an elaborate voodoo ceremony. Lacking a will of their own, these sleepwalking automatons are made to serve the evil master who reanimated them from their graves. These zombie tales introduced the tradition of using the creature as a political statement, as they were a blatant symbol of the evils of slavery.

Although today's zombie tales still have much to say about the problems in our world, they have lost touch with their voodoo history. The zombies your readers are clamoring for in the twenty-first century are more often based on the zombies in George A. Romero's seminal 1968 film, *Night of the Living Dead.*[1] The rules governing the behavior of these ghouls that Romero set out in *Night of the Living Dead* have been incorporated into most zombie literature published since 1968. The zombie story's ground rules are predictable: the dead rise, stumble around brainlessly (known in the zombie business as shambling), relentlessly search for fresh human (or animal) meat to fuel themselves, are grotesquely and partially decayed, can be stopped only by a blow through the brain, can infect living humans, and act only instinctually.

Today's zombies rise from the dead, but they no longer do so through a religious ceremony. Now they are aroused by some kind of plague. "Zombieism" is a kind of virus that infects people and can be passed from the zombie to a healthy human. The infection angle that has entered modern zombie stories is also the key to understanding its appeal with readers. Fans expect these zombies to be portrayed as shambling, unthinking monsters, which clumsily move through a frequently apocalyptic landscape, indiscriminately eating and infecting those in their paths. Although readers find this story line compelling, fans also like that the zombie is a not-so-veiled critique of modern humanity. Zombies can be seen as symbols for the masses, which get "infected" by charismatic politicians or personalities and blindly do as they are told. The dead rise in novels to serve as a cautionary tale for the consequences of blind conformity. Zombies terrify readers because, as a character in George A. Romero's *Day of the Dead* says, "They're us."[2]

In our current stressful economic and political climate, where we have been waging long-standing wars all over the world, a mass zombie uprising does not feel that far from our terrifying realities. This theme underscores the appeal of horror novels as an escape from the true horrors of life. Things may be bad right now, but at least we are not in the middle of a zombie apocalypse. To make their point even more clear, in the past few years, authors have begun sidestepping the symbolism and instead writing novels that link zombies and terrorism directly.

Even in their grotesque glory, zombies are a little bit funny. They are a parody of us. They are slow, stupid, and decaying. They reflect our worst fears about the problems in our world in such an extreme manner that the entire situation can appear a bit ridiculous at times. There is even a popular website that will "zombify" you (www.sonypictures.net/movies/zombieland/zombify/). As a result, zombies frequently appear in many comic horror novels. Librarians working with readers who like zombies on the comic side should also turn to chapter 12, "Comic Horror: Laughing in the Face of Fear," to see those books featuring zombies where the chuckles overpower the screams.

What follows is a list of terrifying novels and story collections that best reflect the current state and popularity of zombie fiction as outlined in this chapter. Think of these as your sure-bet zombie picks.

Adams, John Joseph, ed. *The Living Dead.*

If you want to sample the full range of what zombie fiction has to offer, this anthology is an excellent starting point. With reprinted stories ranging from gross out to thought provoking and including authors as varied as Stephen King, Lisa Morton, Kelly Link, and Sherman Alexie, this collection appeals to a wide audience. Readers will also want the sequel, *The Living Dead 2.*

Bell, Alden. *The Reapers Are the Angels.*

Temple is 15 years old and all alone, living in a post-apocalyptic America, where zombies have taken over. This novel is all about atmosphere. Not only is Temple at risk of being eaten by a zombie, but she is also trying to outrun a man who is trying to kill her. At no moment can Temple, or the reader, rest from the fear, anxiety, and horror that pervade every inch of this slim book. *The Reapers Are the Angels* is best described as Southern Gothic meets psychological suspense, with a heavy dose of zombies. It is an original, heartbreaking, and terrifying novel.

Brooks, Max. *World War Z: An Oral History of the Zombie War.*

In this future, alternative history, Brooks recounts a world war fought against a zombie uprising. This novel is written in a journalistic style as a series of fictional, first-person accounts of the survivors. Readers see firsthand how governments conspired to withhold information; people lost their loved ones to infection and entire societies collapsed, all in a fairly short time. This book's unique construction takes some getting used to, but its intimate style sucks you right into the action and the pure terror.

Fingerman, Bob. *Pariah.*

When a zombie plague wipes out most of humanity, a small band of survivors gathers in a New York City apartment building to hold off the advancing hordes of hungry zombies. Inevitably, however, their supplies begin to dwindle and tempers rise. Their only hope appears to be Mona, a girl whom the zombies never seem to bother. The inclusion of someone who is immune to a zombie plague is new to the subgenre and adds a novel twist to this story. The horrors the survivors inflict upon one another as well as the unsettling ending make *Pariah* a good choice for zombie fans new and old.

Golden, Christopher, ed. *The New Dead: A Zombie Anthology.*

In this solid zombie anthology featuring nineteen original stories by well-known horror writers, readers will be transported beyond the usual barren wastelands of the zombie apocalypse. This noteworthy collection also includes excellent new stories by Joe Hill and Jonathan Maberry, the two biggest names in twenty-first-century horror.

Keene, Brian. *The Rising.*

Keene's fast rise to the top of the genre began when he won the Bram Stoker Award for *The Rising.* This novel is also credited with reinvigorating the zombie novel. Here, after a scientific mishap has created intelligent zombies, Jim leaves the protection of his bomb shelter in West Virginia in an attempt to rescue his son in New Jersey. On his journey Jim meets a priest, a scientist, and an ex-prostitute. They all have interesting backstories and varied motives, but together they must battle the living and the dead in order to survive. Expect bloody zombie hunting, interesting characters, and scary showdowns. *The Rising* is only the first of Keene's many satisfying zombie novels.

Kenyon, Nate. *Sparrow Rock*.
Six teenagers survive a nuclear bomb explosion in an underground bunker. As they await rescue, things go from bad to worse. First, they find out that it may not be an accident that they ended up in the bomb shelter, and then mutant bugs begin turning everyone into zombies. Should they stay locked underground or attempt to make it on the outside? With its combination of claustrophobic tension, zombie fighting action, and a hopeful but unresolved ending, *Sparrow Rock* is a heart-pounding, edge-of-your-seat read for fans of zombies and post-apocalyptic fiction alike.

King, Stephen. *Cell*.
Long known for his hatred of cell phones, King creates a scenario where a pulse sent out through cell phones renders every person using one at that moment a zombie. Struggling comics writer Clayton leads a band of "normies" through this ruined landscape on his search to find his family. This creepy, cautionary tale of technology gone awry is one of King's fastest-paced books. Also try the animal zombies of *Pet Sematary*.

Kirkman, Robert. *The Walking Dead, Book 1: A Continuing Story of Survival Horror*.
This graphic novel series is the most compelling zombie story out right now. Following police officer Rick Grimes and a band of survivors, Kirkman takes a long and graphic look at what a true zombie apocalypse would entail over an extended time frame. These are intimate stories of survival and terror juxtaposed with intense action sequences. The series is also the basis for the popular AMC series of the same name. More graphic novels are discussed in chapter 13.

Lamberson, Gregory. *Desperate Souls*.
Looking for a new zombie angle? Try this one on for size. A drug lord is using zombies to deal his product on the streets of New York City, and Jake Helman is trying to stop them. This is the second book

featuring Helman, and Lamberson appears to have the makings of a long-running series. Zombie fans specifically will also enjoy how *Desperate Souls* pays homage to the zombies' voodoo origins. This fast-paced and bloody tale takes place on the borderland where horror meets the supernatural thriller.

Langan, Sarah. *The Missing.*

When a teacher takes her class of fourth graders to visit a deserted town, they are infected by a disease that turns them into living zombies. They have not died, but they are ravenous for human flesh all the same. As the virus spreads throughout the town, tension builds, and we watch as the characters we come to love succumb to the virus, one after another. It is not pretty, but it is so compelling that it is almost impossible to look away. This is a tense tale with the worst of the gore left to the reader's imagination.

Lebbon, Tim. *Berserk.*

In this truly horrific tale, a grieving father's attempt to locate the body of his dead son leads him to the site of a mass grave where he hopes to find the body. Instead, he comes upon the partially decomposed body of a young girl who is not entirely dead. The father is shocked and dismayed, but the girl seems to be able to speak to him and even to get him to do her bidding. What follows is a suspenseful and violent tale of secrets, grief, and revenge. *Berserk* is a dark and violent book, not for the weak of stomach.

Lindqvist, John Ajvide. *Handling the Undead.*

Building a name for himself as the Swedish Stephen King, Lindqvist tries his hand at the zombie novel to great acclaim. After an unexpected heat wave, the streets of Stockholm are filled with the risen dead. Various characters are followed—some are trying to outrun the zombies and others are hoping their loved ones are reanimated. This is a psychological, character-driven story that brings up questions about the human condition that will haunt readers long after they finish the novel.

Little, Bentley. *The Walking.*

Horror mainstay Little's entry into the subgenre is also one of his best novels. After his father dies and transforms into a "walker"—one of an army of zombies who are instinctively shambling to the remote deserts of Arizona—PI Miles Huerdeen is called into action to discover what ancient evil is responsible for reanimating the dead. A sense of doom permeates the entire novel, as Miles's quest seems more and more hopeless. An interesting twist makes for a satisfying conclusion. Fans of older zombie fiction will enjoy this book.

Maberry, Jonathan. *Rot and Ruin.*

The first book in a projected young adult series, *Rot and Ruin* is a great read for zombie fans of any age. Our protagonist is 15-year-old Benny, who lives in a time only a generation removed from the zombie apocalypse. We enter this post-apocalyptic world through Benny, who is about to become an apprentice zombie killer. There is a lot of detail about how the zombies rose and took over, as well as plenty of character development and action to propel the story into a long-running series. This is an especially good choice for the more squeamish reader who wants to experience the zombie craze.

McKinney, Joe. *Dead City.*

Rising star McKinney asks readers who thought Katrina was bad to imagine surviving five hurricanes in a row, only to find that in the rubble, a virus has been born that is reanimating the dead—thousands of them at a time! Quickly, the virus spreads across the entire state of Texas, as hordes of hungry zombies begin taking over. This is a terrifying and action-packed story with a realistic premise. McKinney returns to the action of *Dead City* in *Apocalypse of the Dead.*

Ochse, Weston. *Empire of Salt.*

Bombay Beach, California, is not a prosperous town; it smells, there are lots of earthquakes, and it is populated by the dregs of civilization. And that doesn't consider the hordes of zombies running rampant. Ochse plays off the common horror setting of the isolated town and then lets the zombies loose. Good, gory zombie fun.

Smith, Bryan. *Deathbringer.*

In the town of Dandridge a figure known as the Deathbringer has been able to alter God's law and reanimate the dead. As people die and come back as zombies, they attack more citizens, causing more death. Soon the zombies outnumber the living. Will anyone survive? This is a great read for people who want some action mixed in with their horror. And, as in all Smith's novels, there is plenty of gore to go around.

Somtow, S. P. *Darker Angels.*

A mysterious, one-eyed voodoo priest ventures to raise dead soldiers from the battlefields of the Civil War in a sweeping novel that features a cast of characters ranging from Edgar Allan Poe, Abraham Lincoln, and Lord Byron to the New Orleans voodoo queen, Marie Laveau. This is a great choice for fans of horror and historical fiction. It is also the only title on the list that explicitly harkens back to the zombies' voodoo origins.

Tripp, Ben. *Rise Again: A Zombie Thriller.*
In a small town outside Los Angeles during a Fourth of July celebration, the crowds start going crazy. A zombie uprising has begun, and the few survivors head north for help. *Rise Again* has great characters, political intrigue, and gory zombie action. Tripp is a great new voice in the genre.

Turner, Joan Frances. *Dust.*
Jessica has been dead for nine years. She is a zombie who can remember her past life and can feel emotions, but is unable to communicate with the living. Things are rough until Jessica joins a zombie gang. Just as her life improves, a strange disease begins to attack humans and zombies. It is at this point that this original, subtle, psychological, and haunting novel really begins.

Wellington, David. Monster Trilogy: *Monster Island, Monster Nation, Monster Planet.*
In this popular trilogy, the story begins a month after a catastrophic event turns the population of Manhattan into insatiable, nasty zombies. The second book goes back to the time before the zombies have taken hold, while the third is set twelve years later, in a world where it seems the zombies have won. The trilogy mixes horror with traditional fantasy elements, such as sorcerers. The compelling, teenage female protagonist has also drawn in more female fans. Wellington has marketed himself well, releasing many of his novels in serial form online for free. Once readers discover this author, they become as ravenous for more books as his zombies are for human flesh.

BECKY'S ZOMBIES PICKS

The Rising, by Brian Keene

The Walking Dead series, by Robert Kirkman

World War Z, by Max Brooks

NOTES

1. George A. Romero, *Night of the Living Dead*, DVD (1968; Culver City, CA: Columbia TriStar Home Video, 1999).
2. Douglas E. Winter, *Prime Evil: New Stories by the Masters of Modern Horror* (New York: New American Library, 1988), 5.

TITLE/AUTHOR LIST

Apocalypse of the Dead, by Joe McKinney

Berserk, by Tim Lebbon

Cell, by Stephen King

Darker Angels, by S. P. Somtow

Dead City, by Joe McKinney

Deathbringer, by Bryan Smith

Desperate Souls, by Gregory Lamberson

Dust, by Joan Frances Turner

Empire of Salt, by Weston Ochse

Handling the Undead, by John Ajvide Lindqvist

The Living Dead, edited by John Joseph Adams

The Living Dead 2, edited by John Joseph Adams

The Missing, by Sarah Langan

Monster Island, by David Wellington

Monster Nation, by David Wellington

Monster Planet, by David Wellington

The New Dead: A Zombie Anthology, edited by Christopher Golden

Pariah, by Bob Fingersmith

Pet Sematary, by Stephen King

The Reapers Are the Angels, by Alden Bell

Rise Again: A Zombie Thriller, by Ben Tripp

The Rising, by Brian Keene

Rot and Ruin, by Jonathan Maberry

Sparrow Rock, by Nate Kenyon

The Walking, by Bentley Little

The Walking Dead, Book 1: A Continuing Story of Survival Horror, by Robert Kirkman

World War Z: An Oral History of the Zombie War, by Max Brooks

8

SHAPE-SHIFTERS
Nature Morphs into Something Terrifying

Throughout history, man has revered and even worshipped animals. The more powerful and predatory the beast, the more respect it tended to elicit. Faced with powerful predators in their midst, people incorporated them into their lore. The threatening animal theme in the horror novel plays off this fear and respect. These books address our primal fear of being attacked by a wild beast or even a domesticated animal. The idea that Fido could become a ferocious killer or that the crows sitting on the wire behind your house could shift into human form is prime fodder for the horror author. And I haven't even mentioned the naturally creepy animals like spiders and snakes, who also regularly organize to wreak havoc in the pages of horror novels.

It is important to note, however, that an animal gone wild story line alone does not automatically make a book a horror novel. Going back to my definition of horror in chapter 2, the creature stalking our heroes must be unearthly. So, a shark gone crazy, as in *Jaws* (Benchley), is not horror, but a man who can change into a wolf and go on a killing spree is (*Sharp Teeth*, Barlow). Also, readers who enjoy this subgenre tend to like books that feature any living thing being transformed into a supernatural killer. Authors have picked up on this preference and have begun to offer many titles with prescient and violent plants.

One of the most fearsome and well-known animals in folklore is the wolf, and certain legends center on lycanthropy, the transformation of a man into a werewolf. Shape-shifting is deeply rooted in folklore and myth throughout the world. The legendary twins Romulus and Remus, who founded Rome, are said to have been nursed by a she-wolf and acquired her ferocity as a result. The folktales of Europe, India, China, and America's Indians are all rich in tales of transformation. In the classic legend of the werewolf, a man who has been bitten by a wolf is periodically transformed (usually under the full moon) into a fur-covered, snarling beast who abandons his humanity for the bestial appearance and behavior of the animal. This animal probably caught the imagination of ancient cultures because throughout much of human history wolf packs were a real menace to rural farmers and their livestock.

Although humans have become more industrialized and moved more into city living, the werewolf tale has stayed with us. So we need to ask, what accounts for the appeal of the shape-shifter story in the twenty-first century? The answer can be found in the appeal of horror itself. The shape-shifting character, whether it is the protagonist, the villain, or both, represents the split within us all. Many shape-shifters want to be good, but the change makes them lose control; they cannot help their evil nature. The appeal of these tales lies in our own fear that we too could lose control of our darkest impulses. We read on in fear and dread, but are fascinated throughout.

The best example of the modern werewolf story is Toby Barlow's *Sharp Teeth*. No longer held hostage to the phases of the moon or forced to hide in the woods, Barlow's urban Los Angeles werewolves can shift at will. This is a complex story of rival wolf packs, battling over their territory and involved in organized crime. Barlow's werewolves are also complex humans with their own desires and needs. Finally, the book's style adds to its appeal. Barlow chose to write *Sharp Teeth* in free verse. Obtrusive at first, the poetry falls into an easy rhythm after a few pages. The most striking result of this stylistic choice is a ragged, unjustified right margin that mimics actual sharp teeth, thus enhancing the menacing tone of the entire work.

Although the shape-shifter holds its own unique appeal, it also shares appeals with all the animals of terror that grace the pages of horror novels. You would be hard-pressed to find an animal that has not been made terrifying by a horror author. The books in this list include the obvious animals of terror such as wolves, spiders, and snakes, but there is also a new biological predator stalking the pages of the horror novel: plants of terror. While these plants of terror have much in common with their cousins in the monster subgenre, their basis in the natural world is the key to their appeal. All the fear invoked by the otherworldly threats in the novels listed in this chapter is initially based on the reader's implicit knowledge that Nature is a powerful force. As much as we humans have learned about the world and as much as we have learned to control the world with technology, we have never been able to conquer Nature. And when that which we cannot control turns evil, how can we stop it from destroying us? This is where our terror begins.

Barlow, Toby. *Sharp Teeth.*

Written in a free verse style in which the pattern created by the ends of the lines creates the illusion of literal sharp teeth, Barlow's novel introduces a new type of werewolf, the urban wolf. This is a gritty story of underground crime and rival packs of werewolves who can morph at will. *Sharp Teeth* has romance, violence, and a compellingly complex story line.

Braunbeck, Gary A. *Keepers.*

In this haunting coming-of-age tale, Gill is warned by a dying man that the Keepers are coming. Almost at once, Gill is plunged into a nightmarish world where strange animals and troubling reminders of the past overwhelm him. But Gill must persevere in order to stop the Keepers from wreaking havoc on the world. This character-centered story is intense and shocking, but extremely satisfying.

Clark, Simon. *The Night of the Triffids.*

Written as a sequel to the 1951 cult classic, *The Day of the Triffids* by John Wyndham, *The Night of the Triffids* looks at life twenty-five years after a walking plant-monster has taken over much of civilization. Here a band of survivors, led by the son of the original book's protagonist, have begun to rebuild civilization on an island. Things are going well until the triffids figure out how to leave the mainland and renew their attack. This is a terrifying story of a post-apocalyptic landscape where death by plant is a very real threat. It is also a great backlist suggestion for your hordes of zombies fans.

Farris, John. *High Bloods.*

A werewolf virus plague is spreading across the world, and the International Lycan Control (ILC) has been set up to keep the infected from terrorizing the uninfected during the full moon. However, a California agent of the ILC notices that the controls may no longer be working. *High Bloods* is a hardboiled horror story that follows a terrifyingly realistic werewolf takeover of the world as we know it.

Gagliani, W. D. *Wolf's Trap.*

Nick Lupo is a no-nonsense cop, but he is also a werewolf. In this Bram Stoker Award–nominated first book in a series, Nick is pursued by Martin, a serial killer who is out for revenge. Although Nick the man is a stand-up guy, Nick the Wolf inadvertently killed Martin's sister while under the change. Nick has to battle Martin as well as the creature inside himself. What follows is a gory, unsettling, and fear-inducing story in which the reader must constantly question the characters' motives. The series continues with *Wolf's Gambit* and *Wolf's Bluff.*

Garton, Ray. *Ravenous.*

In a small California town, vicious werewolves are on the loose, and werewolf hunter Daniel Fargo has come to help. It appears this outbreak of lycanthropy is spread through sexual contact, and once a human contracts this horrid STD, there is no hope. There is nothing sympathetic about these werewolves; they are vicious and without a conscience. Watch out, because the tension is as unrelenting as the violence.

Gonzalez, J. F. *Shapeshifter.*

Mark is a werewolf who is desperately trying to hide his condition and the murderous actions in his past. Bernard is the CEO of a large company who witnesses Mark's shifting on a security camera. Bernard uses the video evidence to blackmail Mark into becoming a contract killer. Readers will be hard-pressed to find sympathy for either man, but the question of who will win this violent battle will engage them in a terrifying drama.

Holland, David. *Murcheston: The Wolf's Tale.*

The Victorian Londoner Edgar Lenoir, Duke of Darnley, loves hunting. After surviving a nasty run-in with a wolf in Carpathia, he finds himself metamorphosing into a wolf and losing his humanity while being consumed with the animal desires of the beast he is to become. Told in an epistolary style that mirrors *Dracula*, *Murcheston* recounts the personal and unsettling tale of Edgar's final journey from man to monster.

Keene, Brian. *The Conqueror Worms.*

A global flood has left Earth devastated. To make matters worse, giant slime-covered holes keep showing up in what land is left. And then, man-eating worms the size of buses begin to attack. But wait, a creature even more horrid than the earthworms comes knocking! To ratchet up the dread even more, the novel is written as a reminiscence of recent events by one of the protagonists as he lies dying. This is an original story, deeply influenced by Lovecraft.

Keene, Brian. *A Gathering of Crows.*

Do you like shape-shifters, but you're sick of werewolves? What about crows? A small town is terrorized by five evil strangers who are able to shift into black crows. Levi, an ex-Amish magician, is only passing through town, but he is also the only one who can stop the carnage. This is a fast-paced, terror-inducing ride, with very evil villains. Fans of Keene will also appreciate the reappearance of Levi from past titles.

Kiernan, Caitlin R. *The Red Tree.*

Sarah moves to rural Rhode Island and finds fragments of a mysterious manuscript written by her new home's former resident, a parapsychologist who was obsessed with an oak tree on the property's periphery. Sarah becomes entangled in the manuscript and risks her life to find out what the tree is hiding. This is a great example of quiet horror; there is very little blood but plenty of chills.

King, Stephen. *Cujo.*

After being bitten by a rabid bat, Cujo, a 200-pound Saint Bernard, comes under the spell of demonic forces and begins terrorizing his owners and a neighboring family. This terrifying tale of a pet gone mad is heightened by the well-told narrative of the lives of its victims. You will never look at your own dog the same way again.

King, Stephen. *Cycle of the Werewolf.*

A Maine werewolf's escapades are recounted in twelve tales, one for each month's full moon. This is a classic werewolf tale, combining well-known legend with King's superior storytelling. Look for the edition with intricate illustrations by Berni Wrightson to enhance your reading experience.

Lamberson, Gregory. *The Frenzy Way.*

A murderer is on the loose in New York City, but it is not a man police captain Mace is chasing, it is a werewolf. Mace and his motley crew of three supernatural investigators track the werewolf and try to stop him before too many people die. This is a fast-paced, terrifyingly bloody but satisfying tale.

Lee, Edward. *Slither.*

It doesn't take much to make the disgusting parasitic trichinosis worm scary, but this version can alter its host's DNA, forcing the infected human to give birth to more worms. This is a terrifying novel filled with plenty of gore and sex. *Slither* is a great suggestion for readers who like their horror on the icky side.

Maberry, Jonathan. *The Wolfman: A Novelization.*

In this novelization of the Oscar-winning film by the same name, horror master Maberry follows the troubled Lawrence as he is forced into a battle against an ancient curse that turns people into murderous wolves when the moon is full. Lawrence must battle his past as well as bloodthirsty wolves in this dark and gory work.

McCammon, Robert. *The Wolf's Hour.*

Michael is a British spy in the final years of World War II, but he is also a werewolf. The story interestingly juxtaposes Michael's bloody youth in 1920s Russia and his current work in occupied Germany. The contrast between his past activities and his current work chasing down Nazis injects drama and action into the plot of this inventive take on the werewolf story. *The Wolf's Hour* was re-released in 2010 and is seeing renewed interest and praise.

Pinborough, Sarah. *Breeding Ground.*

In a small English town, the women are behaving strangely, and no one can figure out why. Soon our hero learns the truth as he sees his girlfriend give birth to man-eating spiders. A small band of survivors escapes to a military base where they begin to hear rumors of other invasions all over the world. Pinborough feeds off the common human fear of spiders, but takes the terror to a whole new, bloody level. In the sequel, *Feeding Ground,* the murderous spiders reach London. Both books are solid choices for fans of animals of terror or apocalyptic horror.

Smith, Bryan. *Soultaker.*

In this combination of the shape-shifting and demonic possession subgenres, Myra is an ancient shape-shifter who has staked her claim to the souls of the men in a small Tennessee town. She has also recruited the women to be her assistants. What will happen when Trey, a high school boy, tries to stop her? This character-focused tale is not for the squeamish.

Smith, Scott. *The Ruins.*

Four American friends on vacation in Cancun, Mexico, befriend a German tourist who convinces them to join the search for his brother, who was last seen on his way to visit some Mayan ruins. The friends soon regret their decision as they quickly find themselves lost in the jungle, stranded on a hill, and stalked by a horrifying monster—a monster with a 100 percent track record of human destruction. This terrifying, original, and gruesome story will make you squirm as you take a second look at your houseplants.

Stableford, Brian M. *The Werewolves of London.*
Bitten by a snake during a visit to a remote area in Egypt, young David finds himself plagued with strange and extravagant visions. Gabriel also possesses similar visionary powers. The two find themselves caught in a secret war between the forces of werewolves, occultists, and fallen angels. The series continues with *The Angel of Pain* and *The Carnival of Destruction*. Although these are older titles, Stableford is still a popular horror and dark fantasy writer, and you will find these werewolf tales lurking on your shelves, just waiting to be suggested to a new generation of ravenous readers.

Strieber, Whitley. *The Forbidden Zone.*
In this homage to Lovecraft, insect-like monsters swarm over a mountain town. Brian is a physicist trying to forget his past and forge a happy life with his new wife. But can he deal with his personal demons and save his town from these awful insects that first mesmerize and then devour their prey? There is plenty of gore here. This backlist title is a great choice for those who squirm at just the idea of bugs.

Wellington, David. *Frostbite: A Werewolf Tale.*
While on an Arctic expedition, Chey is barely scratched by a wolf, but this encounter changes her life forever. She is taken in by Monty, whose link to Chey is more sinister than it first appears. Told in four parts, *Frostbite* is as edgy as it is scary. It is truly a werewolf tale for the millennial generation.

Zeltserman, Dave. *The Caretaker of Lorne Field.*
For 300 years the oldest male child in the Durkin family has been responsible for weeding Lorne Field. But these are not any weeds. They are monsters known as Aukowies, monsters that, if not weeded, will grow to their full form, leave the ground, and destroy the world. Or will they? With no one left to support or believe in him, the current, and aging, caretaker, Jack, is fighting a losing battle to save the world. This is a tightly wound and intense story in which the suspense and tension build to an unsettling conclusion.

BECKY'S SHAPE-SHIFTERS AND ANIMALS OF TERROR PICKS

The Conqueror Worms, by Brian Keene

The Ruins, by Scott Smith

Sharp Teeth, by Toby Barlow

TITLE/AUTHOR LIST

The Angel of Pain, by Brian M. Stableford

Breeding Ground, by Sarah Pinborough

The Caretaker of Lorne Field, by Dave Zeltserman

The Carnival of Destruction, by Brian M. Stableford

The Conqueror Worms, by Brian Keene

Cujo, by Stephen King

Cycle of the Werewolf, by Stephen King

Feeding Ground, by Sarah Pinborough

The Forbidden Zone, by Whitley Strieber

The Frenzy Way, by Gregory Lamberson

Frostbite: A Werewolf Tale, by David Wellington

A Gathering of Crows, by Brian Keene

High Bloods, by John Farris

The Keepers, by Gary A. Braunbeck

Murcheston: The Wolf's Tale, by David Holland

The Night of the Triffids, by Simon Clark

Ravenous, by Ray Garton

The Red Tree, by Caitlin R. Kiernan

The Ruins, by Scott Smith

Shapeshifter, by J. F. Gonzalez

Sharp Teeth, by Toby Barlow

Slither, by Edward Lee

Soultaker, by Bryan Smith

The Werewolves of London, by Brian M. Stableford

The Wolfman: A Novelization, by Jonathan Maberry

Wolf's Bluff, by W. D. Gagliani

Wolf's Gambit, by W. D. Gagliani

The Wolf's Hour, by Robert McCammon

Wolf's Trap, by W. D. Gagliani

9

MONSTERS AND ANCIENT EVIL
Cthulhu Comes Calling

Anyone who is anyone in horror has a monster story to tell. The monster may be of ancient origin or it may be newly born, but make no mistake, it is out to kill. Monsters have been a part of the human storytelling tradition from its inception. The proof can be seen in the large quantities of monstrous creatures one finds in the mythologies and religions of just about every culture. These monsters were most often created to help our ancestors explain the unexplainable. By injecting an amoral, supernatural being into their stories, humans were able to explain horrible occurrences such as plagues, wars, storms, fires, and earthquakes before they gained the scientific knowledge and vocabulary to do so. Today's horror monster stories tend to focus on a homicidal monster, in a grotesque form, that wrecks havoc on a small town and its troubled residents.

The monsters I will be focusing on are mainly influenced by the two deceased horror authors H. P. Lovecraft and Richard Laymon. Widely considered the most important writer of supernatural horror fiction of the twentieth century, Lovecraft made his mark by writing stories and novellas that abandoned the demons, ghosts, and vampires of his predecessors. Instead, Lovecraft created his own distinct universe of legends and mythology, filled with some of the most memorable monsters ever created.[1] Known collectively as the Cthulhu Mythos, these works imagined that alien monsters were trying to take possession of our world. The monster subgenre was defined and popularized through Lovecraft's tales. In the years since his death in 1937, Lovecraft's influence and importance have only grown. References to the author and his works can be seen all over the horror landscape, from websites to novels to movies. For more detailed information about the life and influence of Lovecraft, look to the work of Lovecraft scholar S. T. Joshi.[2]

More recently, the modern monster master is the late Richard Laymon. Laymon's monsters were quite different from Lovecraft's, however. Although a Lovecraftian monster was often functioning on a higher level than the humans it was trying to overtake, Laymon's monsters tended to be grotesque and lumbering beasts, with very little higher brain function beyond survival instincts. He often employed the idea of de-evolution, writing about creatures who may have once been human but have moved backward, becoming savage primates. His monster novels also include a high level of sex and violence. There are rapes and bloody dismemberments. But as long as readers can stomach the gore, they are in for one amazingly scary ride. Thankfully, most of Laymon's novels were previously published overseas, so they are still being released in America. Fans can still get a "new" Laymon novel each year.

Although these two influential authors wrote about different types of monsters, the characteristics they created and developed have had a large influence on the genre. Today's monster story writers grew up reading these authors, and they often reference Lovecraft and Laymon, both intentionally and subconsciously. Being familiar with these two classic authors will help you to better understand the appeal of today's monster novels.

Beyond the influence of Lovecraft and Laymon, there are other issues you should consider when working with readers in this subgenre. First, for many readers, the monsters they most crave are of the ancient variety. This story line generally begins with an archeologist, either professional or volunteer, working on a dig and inadvertently uncovering an ancient evil. The most common examples of these monsters in horror novels are mummies, golems, and South American monsters. The draw here goes beyond the heart-pounding chase. This monster has its basis in folklore, and its discovery by scientists makes it feel more real. The setup seems probable. The "it could really happen" factor adds to the dread. It plays off our belief in the supernatural by legitimizing the horror. As a result, readers may express a preference for stories of ancient evil. Where appropriate I have noted the distinction to help you to assist these readers more easily.

Second, it is important to note that monster stories tend to be set in a small, isolated, or remote area. Isolation is often an essential element in a successful monster story. Why? The monsters can more believably exist in an isolated location; it is easier to explain how the creature went unnoticed for so long. The isolation also enhances the fear. The monster has gone unchecked, the humans are trapped by their remote location, and no one but our flawed and reluctant hero can save the day. In this subgenre you will also see many story lines that involve attacks that have happened before. This further enhances the dread and terror. We are in a place where monsters regularly wreak havoc. So when you hear horror patrons talking about their enjoyment of "small town horror," or they regularly mention how much they enjoyed an isolated setting, this subgenre should be your first stop for suggesting titles.

Another draw of the monster story for horror fans comes from the reader's psyche. In many of these novels, the protagonist is battling his or her inner demons. The monster is there to enhance this inner struggle, as it represents a physical manifestation of the conflict raging inside our hero, a conflict the reader can often sympathize with. Although personal demons are scary, add a homicidal monster to the mix and you move into pure terror. This appeal often is used to add complexity to the monster's motivations, too. The following list encompasses a variety of situations, but the overall message is the same: the monsters here are not simple manifestations of pure evil; they each have a complex story behind their rage.

Finally, it is important to note that these are bloody books. Many include quite graphic descriptions. Readers who are already fans of the subgenre will probably not mention the gore since it is so pervasive. Taken as a group, the books in this subgenre will contain the most sex and violence of any of the books mentioned in this text. Moreover, this violence can lead to the death of a major character. No one is safe in the monster book, and this fact alone, more than the gore, may be enough to keep some readers away from the subgenre. On the other hand, for many readers this peek into an illicit world ruled by revenge, murder, and mayhem is one of the most important appeal factors fueling the continued interest in the monster and ancient evil story.

Braunbeck, Gary. *Far Dark Fields.*

Part of Braunbeck's Cedar Hill mythos, *Far Dark Fields* introduces English teacher Geoff, wracked with guilt after he survived a killing spree in which his family was massacred. He is forced to face his past when the perpetrator of a school shooting asks to speak his dying words to Geoff. These events lead Geoff back to Cedar Hill where he must confront the monster who has been stalking the children of this small Ohio town for years. This is a creepy story of a murder in a town where the supernatural regularly intrudes.

Campbell, Ramsey. *Creatures of the Pool.*

British horror master Campbell follows Gavin in his search for his missing father. While delving into his father's research, Gavin uncovers some terrifying, centuries-old secrets about his hometown. Secrets, suspense, and the supernatural collide in this creepy tale. Also try *The Grin of the Dark* for a creepy ancient evil tale featuring a clown. Campbell can be counted on for a new and satisfying horrific read every year.

Clark, Simon. *This Rage of Echoes.*

What would you do if you were attacked by a monster that looks just like you? Mason has been a victim of the Echomen, body snatchers who can turn people into murderous monsters. Can Mason stop their bloody plans before those he loves become victims? *This Rage of Echoes* plays off our modern fear of identity theft to horrifyingly realistic results.

Clegg, Douglas. *You Come When I Call You.*

A group of friends is forever haunted by what happened to them in the summer of 1980. In an attempt to save themselves, the boys performed a ritual that set in motion horrific events. Twenty years later, the friends have to confront the monster that has been waiting for them. In chapters alternating between past and present, Clegg methodically adds details to the story until the action and the fear spiral out of control. The tension is almost as terrifying as the monster.

Delaney, Matthew. *Jinn.*

In this mystery-horror hybrid, a soldier witnesses a monster breaking out of the stomach of a dead comrade during World War II. The story flashes forward to the twenty-first century where two Boston detectives are investigating a particularly brutal series of murders. This is a fast-paced, investigative story with lots of twists and turns and a monster that lives up to its horror billing.

Due, Tananarive. *My Soul to Keep.*

A 500-year-old African immortal man is living in modern times as David, a jazz scholar in a middle-class family. He has had many lives and loves throughout his long existence, but his current situation as husband to Jessica and father to young Kira is extremely satisfying. However, voices from his ancient past are calling David back to do their bidding. We are both drawn to and frightened by David the man and David the monster. We wait and watch nervously throughout the book. This is a chilling backlist title that I still put in patrons' hands on a regular basis. It has yet to disappoint. Also try *The Good House.*

Dunbar, Robert. *The Pines.*

In the mysterious and desolate New Jersey Pine Barrens, a legendary monster, the Jersey Devil, is on the loose. This is a traditional story of a monster on the prowl in an isolated setting, but Dunbar manages to keep the plot and action fresh, frightening, and fun. Do not go camping soon after reading this book. The Jersey Devil returns to stalk new victims in *The Shore.*

Farris, John. *You Don't Scare Me.*

Chase was almost killed by her evil stepfather, Crow, as a teen, but now, as a student at Yale working on research into new dimensions, she finds Crow is still alive in the Netherworld she has discovered. Crow is more than a ghost; he has become a monster, obsessed with destroying Chase and all she holds dear. This novel by an established voice in horror is a frightening ride. With its compelling thriller and science fiction aspects, *You Don't Scare Me* is sure to appeal to a wide range of readers.

Grant, Charles. *The Black Carousel.*

A master of the macabre, Grant sets this collection of four stories at a carnival. Each of the four protagonists visits the black carousel, and each is forever changed by the ride. The ride itself is the monster here. As the stories come one after another, the awful power of the carousel is revealed, yet we are riveted by the events that result from its power. You will finish the book begging Grant for one more ride.

Keene, Brian. *Castaways.*

A television crew and the contestants in a *Survivor*-esque reality show are literally caught in a fight for their lives—the island they have been left on is populated by an indigenous tribe of bloodthirsty monsters! *Castaways* is a grisly, disturbing, and compelling page-turner. Also try *Ghoul.*

Ketchum, Jack. *She Wakes.*

The streets of Greece are filled with a history both beautiful and terrible. Ketchum mines its mythology to explore what would happen if a vengeful goddess returned to modern Greece to terrorize its people. This thoroughly modern horror novel is a must-read for fans of classical monsters.

Laymon, Richard. *The Woods Are Dark.*

The forests surrounding a small town are the domain of a cannibalistic family of humanoid monsters. The novel recounts, in graphic detail, the experiences of three different groups of hikers as they encounter these terrible monsters. With a 2008 reprint, *The Woods Are Dark* is a great introduction to the shocking and frightening imagination of this horror master. Also don't miss *The Beast House* and the mummies of *To Wake the Dead.*

Lee, Edward. *The Golem.*

The golem was originally an enchanted monster, forged of clay to protect persecuted Jews, but in Lee's hands, new, murderous, evil golems have risen and are stalking a small Maryland town. The mythology behind the golem has been the fodder for folktales and horror stories for hundreds of years, but, in Lee's hands, the monster takes on a more terrifying and bloodthirsty persona.

Little, Bentley. *The Return.*

When archeologists in Arizona begin digging up strange artifacts, an ancient evil is reawakened. Tied to the mythology of the Anasazi people, who were contemporaries of the Maya, this ancient force asserts its power by turning humans and animals upon themselves. Graphic murders, cannibalism, and general mayhem become the norm. This is a horrifying tale of a monster based in Native American folklore.

Maberry, Jonathan. *Ghost Road Blues.*

Thirty years ago, the citizens of Pine Deep, Pennsylvania, killed a serial killer known as the Reaper. Since then, the town has known peace and fame. While the residents get ready for the annual Halloween festival, a new supernatural evil lurks on the outskirts of town, waiting to finish what the Reaper began. The Pine Deep Trilogy includes *Dead Man's Song* and *Bad Moon Rising.* The entire trilogy begs to be read back-to-back-to-back. With the Pine Deep novels' compelling characters, horrific monsters (both human and speculative), and gripping pacing, Maberry has perfectly captured everything horror readers love about the monster story.

Masterton, Graham. *Basilisk.*

Medical researcher Nathan Underhill is trying to genetically engineer a mythological creature to help cure chronically ill people. Although his trials fail, it appears someone else has succeeded, and now an actual basilisk is on the loose, killing everyone who stands in its way. Can Nathan stop the evil creature in time? Readers will be drawn to Masterton's compelling version of ancient evil meeting the mad scientist.

Partridge, Norman. *Dark Harvest.*

It's Halloween in 1963, and the local boys are taking part in their town's traditional hunt to find the October Boy. This is no ordinary hunt, however. The boys must be locked away without food for five days before being let out for the hunt, and he who manages to kill the monster gets a big reward. Readers follow Pete on this particular hunt, and together we find out the horrifying truth behind the ritual. *Dark Harvest* is a critically acclaimed, original, and shocking story that monster fans should not miss.

Peretti, Frank E. *Monster.*

In this horror novel with religious undertones, Peretti warns against science tinkering with God's creations. When Reed and his wife, Beck, are attacked by vicious creatures in the wilderness, Reed escapes but Beck goes missing. Gathering a team to find his wife, Reed not only finds the monsters but uncovers the evil masterminds behind their existence. Equal parts thought provoking and chilling, *Monster* is a good choice for a wide audience.

Saul, John. *The Presence.*

Leaving behind New York City for a quieter life in Hawaii, archeologist and mother Katherine Sundquist becomes witness to an alien life force that almost kills her son and threatens to take over Earth. This novel blends science fiction, thriller, and horror and includes a chilling afterword in which Saul presents the scientific realities that spawned this novel of terror. Most libraries will find this backlist monster tale already lurking on their shelves waiting to attack an unsuspecting reader.

Searcy, David. *Last Things.*

In a small East Texas town, bad things keep happening. A loner, Luther, knows that these occurrences are the work of a supernatural force, but can he stop the malevolent monster on his own? Described as "sophisticated" horror, *Last Things* uses three-dimensional characters, a meticulously built creepy atmosphere, and lyrical prose to provoke readers into feelings of pure terror.

Sigler, Scott. *Ancestor.*

On an isolated island in the middle of Lake Superior, a biotech firm is trying to re-create the ancestor of all mammals in order to use the creature as a universal source of transplantable organs. However, since this is a horror novel, things do not go smoothly, and soon the island is awash in bloody, relentless action. Great characters and a truly frightening monster make this a compelling read.

Simmons, Dan. *The Terror.*

Simmons adds a supernatural twist in this historical novel of Sir John Franklin's mysterious and failed 1840s arctic search for the Northwest Passage. No one knows what really happened after the ships became trapped in the ice, but Simmons's description of disease, cannibalism, and a monstrous creature stalking the crew is compelling and terrifying. This is an intricately plotted story with an oppressively menacing atmosphere. Also try the backlist title, *Summer of Night.*

Smith, Bryan. *Depraved.*

The small town of Hopkins Bend is filled with monstrous creatures, and outsiders who visit rarely make it out alive. When a group of young travelers stumbles upon the town, they find they may have been brought there as a sacrifice to the monster who rules all. Reader beware: this novel is filled with graphic violence and sex in doses higher than normal even for this already graphic subgenre, but those who take the plunge will be hard-pressed to tear themselves away from the story.

Strand, Jeff. *Dweller.*

Toby is an outcast who finds peace in the deep woods behind his home. He also finds a monster living there—a monster named Owen, who becomes Toby's best friend for over fifty years. But when your best friend is an actual monster, he can inflict horrible things on your enemies. This is an original, heart-breaking, and chilling story.

Straub, Peter. *Floating Dragon.*

This tale of suburban horror has a little bit of everything between its covers, but ultimately it is the story of a town, its inhabitants, and the supernatural killer who has been stalking them for over 300 years. If you cannot decide what horror subgenre to start with, pick up *Floating Dragon* to get a little taste of it all by one of the genre's best writers.

BECKY'S MONSTER PICKS

Castaways, by Brian Keene

Ghost Road Blues, by Jonathan Maberry

My Soul to Keep, by Tananarive Due

NOTES

1. "H. P. Lovecraft," *Contemporary Authors Online* (Detroit: Gale, 2007) and *Literature Resource Center* (accessed December 2, 2010).

2. S. T. Joshi has written numerous books and articles about Lovecraft, but new readers should start with *H. P. Lovecraft: A Life* (West Warwick, RI: Necronomicon Press, 1996). Joshi has edited collections of Lovecraft's stories as well as the author's personal letters. He has also written a few biographies of the author, including *H. P. Lovecraft* (Mercer Island, WA: Starmont House, 1982).

TITLE/AUTHOR LIST

Ancestor, by Scott Sigler

Bad Moon Rising, by Jonathan Maberry

Basilisk, by Graham Masterton

The Beast House, by Richard Laymon

The Black Carousel, by Charles Grant

Castaways, by Brian Keene

Creatures of the Pool, by Ramsey Campbell

Dark Harvest, by Norman Partridge

Dead Man's Song, by Jonathan Maberry

Depraved, by Bryan Smith

Dweller, by Jeff Strand

Far Dark Fields, by Gary A. Braunbeck

Floating Dragon, by Peter Straub

Ghost Road Blues, by Jonathan Maberry

Ghoul, by Brian Keene

The Golem, by Edward Lee

The Good House, by Tananarive Due

The Grin of the Dark, by Ramsey Campbell

Jinn, by Matthew Delaney

Last Things, by David Searcy

Monster, by Frank E. Peretti

My Soul to Keep, by Tananarive Due

The Pines, by Robert Dunbar

The Presence, by John Saul
The Return, by Bentley Little
She Wakes, by Jack Ketchum
The Shore, by Robert Dunbar
Summer of Night, by Dan Simmons
The Terror, by Dan Simmons
This Rage of Echoes, by Simon Clark
To Wake the Dead, by Richard Laymon
The Woods Are Dark, by Richard Laymon
You Come When I Call You, by Douglas Clegg
You Don't Scare Me, by John Farris

10

WITCHES AND THE OCCULT
Double, Double, Toil and Trouble

A person who practices occult arts may go by many names, but the most common is simply "witch." Across cultures and over the course of recorded human history, there are always people who claim to be able to harness magic both to help their community and sometimes to hinder it. There are black-robed, stoop-shouldered hags coexisting with New Age herbalists, Celtic druids, and fairy-tale Disney depictions of both good and bad sorcerers. Shakespeare's tempestuous witch sisters mesh with our memories of *The Crucible* and *The Blair Witch Project,* and even the British wizard-in-training, Harry Potter. More often than not, witches and their powers have been associated with negative images. They use charms, potions, and curses. Some are mischievous and bring ill fortune to others, and they belong to covens that hold services under cover of darkness to discuss their magic and pay homage to their master, the Devil. Despite this diversity, the one uniform distinction of all witches is the element of magic. All have some sort of magical or mystical ability to manipulate the forces of nature.

Witches have been putting their dark curses on people in literature for thousands of years, but the question here is, why are they still popular with twenty-first-century readers? Much of the interest in witch tales stems from their connection to a specific place. In this subgenre, authors tend to focus on two specific settings. The first is tied to the Western world's obsession with persecuting those accused of witchcraft. Organized religion has demonized witchcraft for much of its history. This practice culminated in putting witches on trial, most memorably in America, in Salem, Massachusetts, during the late seventeenth century. As a result, many American horror novelists tend to set their witch stories in New England

and include the reawakening of a persecuted witch out for revenge. Readers enjoy the mingling of true events and fictional supposition they find in the books in this subgenre. A good example of this type of book is *Grimm Memorials* by R. Patrick Gates.

The second popular setting for witch tales is New Orleans. With its history of black magic, Louisiana has become a popular place to let witches run wild. Anne Rice's novels serve as the perfect example here. With *The Witching Hour,* Rice introduced us to the Mayfair Witches, a multigenerational family of witches living in the Garden District of New Orleans. The series traces the family for four centuries up to the 1990s. With strong ties to Gothic tradition, Rice's witches are ancients passing their art down through their lineage to descendants coming to terms with their magical abilities. She also drew upon the black magic prominent in the history of New Orleans. Rice's witches may not have been subjected to burning at the stake like the witches of Salem, but they are also part of a rich tradition. Rice's compelling characters, who question their powers even as they are causing destruction, have entranced a generation of readers, and her influence is still felt in authors such as Deborah LeBlanc. Although the titles in this series are no longer "new," their influence is seen in twenty-first-century titles, and, most important, they are still regularly sought by readers.

Today's readers of witch horror love the fear induced by one of the specific settings just mentioned, but they are also willing to encounter a witch elsewhere. More often than not, readers will find horrific witches in isolated settings, the most common of which seems to be a secluded forest. Isolated settings always increase the tension and fear in horror, but add the appeal of witchcraft and its dark history, and the reader's heart starts racing from the opening lines. *Dark Mountain* by Richard Laymon is an excellent example of an isolated forest being expertly mined for intense terror. So whether it is New England, New Orleans, or the creepy forest on the outskirts of town, readers are craving an occult ceremony and the release of an evil force in a place just outside the normal boundaries of their everyday life.

Beyond setting, two other appeal factors draw in today's witch readers. First, fans of this subgenre have a general interest in witchcraft, the intrigue and fear associated with such powers, and the witch's ability to easily hide among us. As they read, the fear produced by knowing that their neighbor or friend could be a witch in disguise, conjuring black magic spirits without attracting notice, is terrifying. The emergence of Wicca as a modern witchcraft-based religion has also helped to fuel this fear. Authors use their readers' fascination with witchcraft to their advantage by increasing their use of the witch hiding among us in their works.

Second, readers crave these stories of the occult because in a world filled with war and economic uncertainty, it is both terrifying and perversely comforting to know a simple spell recited by a purveyor of magic can either turn everything around or bring it all crashing down. The terror is both enchanting and frightening in the modern witch story. This is an irresistible combination for any horror fan

The list that follows includes books that reflect these appeal factors for today's readers. You will find the most recent witch stories in the horror genre and some key tales from the past. This list shows the draw of history on both the authors and readers of these stories. Although witches are gaining in popularity in horror titles as investigators and romantic leads, the titles here focus on the havoc and terror the evil witch can wreak. Therefore, the first goal of the novels in this list is to create a feeling of intense fear; from that, a compelling story follows.

Buchan, John. *Witch Wood.*

Set in the seventeenth century, this novel plays off the old Scottish tradition of witch tales. A minister is trying to protect his congregation from a coven of devil worshippers; however, over the course of the story, his loyalties become divided. This backlist title has seen renewed interest and is back in print. *Witch Wood* combines adventure, internal struggles, religion, and witchcraft. It is a scary choice for readers new to witch tales.

Campbell, Ramsey. *The Darkest Part of the Woods.*

In this moody story of a haunted English wood, a family is torn apart by its connection to the forest. The history of the wood is linked to an alchemist who lived in the forest and tried to summon an evil spirit. With a nod to *The Blair Witch Project,* a new generation of the family tries not to go mad discovering the wood's secrets. This is a modern story of inescapable horror grounded in classical roots. Campbell's *Pact of the Fathers* is also a solid witch novel.

Clegg, Douglas. *Naomi.*

In this character-centered, fast-paced story, Jake is searching for his lost love, Naomi, in New York City, but when Naomi commits suicide, her spirit needs Jake's help to uncover an evil that is lurking in the subway tunnels under the city. The story moves between modern events and colonial times with witches and witchcraft playing key parts in the conflict. This is a must-read for any horror fan by a master of modern horror. In an interesting side note, *Naomi* was the Internet's first publisher-sponsored e-serial novel.

Dziemianowicz, Stefan R., Robert H. Weinberg, and Martin H. Greenberg, eds. *100 Wicked Little Witch Stories.*

This well-compiled collection goes out of its way to include stories about every kind of witch. The stories range from truly terrifying to charming, with every emotion in between. It is the perfect book for witch fans. *The Ultimate Witch,* a collection edited by Byron Preiss and John Betancourt, is also a good choice for those looking for a short story collection focused on witches and black magic.

Everson, John. *Sacrifice.*

Ariana is a witch who is devoted to conjuring a race of evil spirits known as the Curbine. A group of reluctant heroes is in a race to stop Ariana from destroying the world. This is a sexy, violent, and terrifying novel with frenetic pacing that stands as a solid example of the best of today's horror. You could also try Everson's *Covenant* and *Siren* for more witch-inspired horror.

Gates, R. Patrick. *Grimm Memorials.*

In an attempt to live a simpler life, the Nailer family leaves Boston to move to the quiet New England woods. Little do they know that they are about to encounter Eleanor, the evil witch who has enchanted the residents of their new town and is stealing their children to sacrifice for her magic ceremonies. This is a chilling horror novel with fairy tale roots, sure to appeal to a wide audience. Also try *Grimm Reapings.*

Goshgarian, Gary. *The Stone Circle.*

Widower Peter Van Zandt, an archeology professor, supervises an excavation on an island in Boston Harbor that uncovers stones reminiscent of Stonehenge. But these stones and their black magic are causing Peter's nightmares and real life to merge into a terrifying blur. *The Stone Circle* is a solid example of a compelling witching read that you may have forgotten about. This is also a good suggestion for John Saul fans who are looking for something new.

Gustainis, Justin. *Black Magic Woman.*

This genre-crossing first book of a series following paranormal investigators Morris and Chastain is set in contemporary time, but it is our world with monsters running amok. Here Morris and Chastain must stop a witch with a centuries-old grudge. This series is more horrific than paranormal, as the main goal of Gustainis is to invoke terror. This is a scary story with great characters, a powerfully evil witch, and a quickly escalating pace that will appeal to many horror fans.

Joyce, Graham. *Dark Sister.*

Maggie finds a witch's diary in her home's old fireplace. With it she discovers her own powers and unleashes the Dark Sister, a malevolent force threatening her sanity and her family's well-being. This is an award-winning, terrifying witch tale that will make you squirm without any gore. It is a great example of atmospheric horror—a book that builds the tension to intense fear without any blood being spilled.

Kenyon, Nate. *Bloodstone.*

Ex-con Billy and the prostitute he kidnapped are plagued by evil dreams as they pull into White Falls, Maine. In the town, a young boy named Jed is entranced by a 300-year-old magical amulet. Thrown together by the influence of the cursed necklace, the characters engage in an epic showdown between good and evil. This is a character-driven novel, obviously influenced by Stephen King, with a consciously building pace and a surprising twist. *Bloodstone* was the debut novel of one of today's best horror voices.

Laymon, Richard. *Dark Mountain.*

Two families go on a camping trip to a mountainous forest. What should be a peaceful and restful vacation turns horrifying as they encounter a witch who places a curse on both families. After returning home, the families find the curse is all too real, and to overturn it, some of them must go back to the forest. In pure Laymon form, this is a terrifying and bloody story of a frighteningly realistic witch bent on destruction. Think twice about reading this novel before your next camping trip.

LeBlanc, Deborah. *Water Witch.*

Dunny is a Louisiana witch who has lived her life as an outcast. But when a Native American who can invoke the spirits of his people begins kidnapping children, Dunny is enlisted to use her powers to help stop the conjured ghosts and the Indian witch from continuing their reign of terror. This is a compelling good witch versus bad witch novel by one of the best female horror writers today.

Leiber, Fritz. *Conjure Wife.*

Norman Saylor, a professor of sociology, discovers that his wife, Tansy, practices witchcraft to ward off ill luck and evil influences. When Norman demands that Tansy quit sorcery, their lives fall apart, and he is forced to put his prejudices aside and learn the skills of conjuring magic. Originally written in 1953, with numerous reissues in the intervening years, *Conjure Wife* is now considered a classic in the subgenre by authors and readers alike.

Masterton, Graham. *The 5th Witch.*

In Los Angeles, mobsters and a 350-year-old witch, Rebecca, take the city hostage by violently overthrowing the police. Rebecca is strong. Not only can she be in five places at once, but she also has a stable of witches from all over the world helping her. Detective Dan Fisher fights this black magic by enlisting the help of his neighbor, good witch Anne Conjure. Together, they try to save their city from Rebecca's reign of terror, destruction, and murder. Masterton has become the master at blending horror with thriller elements, creating novels that are scary and compelling rides for his readers.

Maugham, W. Somerset. *The Magician.*

A young surgeon struggles against the wealthy and sinister Oliver Haddo, a practitioner of black magic, who has a perverse attraction to the doctor's beautiful fiancé. This is a classic tale of good versus evil that will leave you spellbound. *The Magician* is still in print and makes for a good addition to any general horror collection.

Mitchell, Mary Ann. *The Witch.*

Cathy, an unhappy witch, commits suicide, only to have her son, Stephen, use witchcraft to bring her back. But Cathy does not want to be back, and she begins to use her powers and her band of demons to wreck havoc on everyone who ever hurt her in life. This is a plot-driven and shocking novel of revenge. Don't be deceived by the mother-son bond; Cathy is pure evil incarnate.

Mostert, Natasha. *Season of the Witch.*

When Gabriel agrees to help track down a missing man, he encounters two beautiful witches who are out to seduce him. But Gabriel has his own secret—he can read people's minds. This is a beguiling and frightening story of witchcraft, memory, and mystery. Filled with twists and intriguing characters, Mostert's novel moves surprisingly quickly through its 400-plus pages.

Passarella, J. G. *Wither.*

Three hundred years ago, three women were hanged as witches in Windale, Massachusetts. Wendy Ward performs a ritual in the 1990s that goes awry, unwittingly freeing the three witches. Wendy must reverse what she has started before she is drawn into the evil. *Wither* won a Bram Stoker Award for best first novel. Readers will be drawn to Wendy and her plight to beat the powerful witches.

Piccirilli, Tom. *A Choir of Ill Children.*

Thomas is a descendant of his backwoods swamp town's founders. He is also the guardian of his conjoined triplet brothers, who share a brain and act as an oracle. When an outsider comes to town, dark secrets are revealed, a coven of witches is upset, and an odd preacher begins speaking in tongues. Thomas must take control and find out the truth. This is a creepy novel, filled with rich and macabre characters, written in a conscious Southern Gothic style.

Rice, Anne. Mayfair Witches (in series order).

The Witching Hour

Rowan Mayfair returns to New Orleans for her mother's funeral only to discover her family's shocking history, which spans four centuries of Mayfair Witches, and the family's powerful influence over and connections to a spirit named Lasher.

Lasher

Rowan Mayfair, queen of a coven of witches, flees the compelling, irresistible Lasher, who attempts to create a child strong enough for his spirit to inhabit.

Taltos

Ashlar, a member of a giant, humanlike race, teams up with the Mayfair Witches to thwart whoever is killing their mutual friends.

Saul, John. *Black Creek Crossing.*

Angel is an outcast teenager who lives in a haunted house. With the help of her only friend, Seth, she uncovers a book of spells that belonged to the home's original owners. Angel and Seth use the spells to torment the bullies at school, but little do they know that an evil force is pulling all the strings. How long until Angel and Seth become the next victims? Reader beware: although Seth and Angel are sympathetic, they do not get away with their use of witchcraft unscathed. This is a satisfying horror novel by a modern master.

Straub, Peter. *A Dark Matter.*

In 1966 four friends participated in an occult ceremony that had gruesome consequences. Now adults, they come together to recount their experiences, realizing that their childhood game might have unleashed an evil force into the world. Straub mentions more blood and gore than he shows here, as he introduces the terrifying idea that all hope is lost. This newer title is garnering this established author some of the highest praise of his distinguished career. *Shadowland* is also a solid entry in this subgenre.

BECKY'S WITCHES PICKS

A Dark Matter, by Peter Straub

Naomi, by Douglas Clegg

Sacrifice, by John Everson

TITLE/AUTHOR LIST

100 Wicked Little Witch Stories, edited by Stefan R. Dziemianowicz, Robert H. Weinberg, and Martin H. Greenberg

Black Creek Crossing, by John Saul

Black Magic Woman, by Justin Gustainis

Bloodstone, by Nate Kenyon

A Choir of Ill Children, by Tom Piccirilli

Conjure Wife, by Fritz Leiber

Covenant, by John Everson

A Dark Matter, by Peter Straub

Dark Mountain, by Richard Laymon

Dark Sister, by Graham Joyce

The Darkest Part of the Woods, by Ramsey Campbell

The 5th Witch, by Graham Masterton

Grimm Memorials, by R. Patrick Gates

Grimm Reapings, by R. Patrick Gates

Lasher, by Anne Rice

The Magician, by W. Somerset Maugham

Naomi, by Douglas Clegg

Pact of the Fathers, by Ramsey Campbell

Sacrifice, by John Everson

Season of the Witch, by Natasha Mostert

Shadowland, by Peter Straub

Siren, by John Everson

The Stone Circle, by Gary Goshgarian

Taltos, by Anne Rice

The Ultimate Witch, edited by Byron Preiss and John Betancourt

Water Witch, by Deborah LeBlanc

The Witch, by Mary Ann Mitchell

Witch Wood, by John Buchan

The Witching Hour, by Anne Rice

Wither, by J. G. Passarella

11

SATAN AND DEMONIC POSSESSION
The Devil Inside

Satan, Lucifer, Beelzebub—whatever we choose to call him, the Devil is a universal symbol of evil throughout Western culture. Therefore, it is not surprising that stories which revolve around the Prince of Darkness comprise an entire subgenre of horror literature. Any time the Devil is invoked in a story, people become frightened and brace themselves for horrible things to start happening. This gut instinct on the reader's part makes it easy for the horror author to create an atmosphere of terror around a tale of demonic possession or satanism. But because stories of people selling their souls to the Devil or children being possessed are fairly common, the author also has to go out of his or her way to make the work fresh and original. As a result, the best novels in this subgenre not only deal with the Devil but also force the protagonists (and by extension the readers) to take a long, hard look at themselves, specifically at their flaws and failings.

One can expect to find four basic plots or story lines in the works in this subgenre: demonic possession, satanic ritual, the curse or the cursed object, and, of course, the selling of one's soul to the Devil. Each of these broad categories has its own characteristics, but the appeal for the entire subgenre is pretty standard. Moreover, some of the best books in this subgenre include elements of all four story lines.

In the stories of demonic possession, a person, usually an innocent child, is possessed by the Devil himself, one of his disciples, or an extremely evil person. Although any novel that explores issues revolving around Satan has an underlying religious element, possession tales tend to tackle this element in a much more direct manner. Priests and clergymen are common characters as they assist in exorcising the demon from the possessed. These representatives of organized religion are not always seen in the best light, as authors commonly use the demonic possession tale to satirize the clergy and organized religion. Satan takes hold despite their presence, and they have to scramble to banish him. However, though the exorcism is usually successful in these tales, the Devil is never gone; he is simply biding his time until he can strike again.

The most important work in this category is *The Exorcist* by William Peter Blatty. Discussed in more detail in chapter 4, "The Classics: Time-Tested Tales of Terror," *The Exorcist* has become the modern standard for all possession tales. It is a testament to Blatty's imagination and writing skills that despite its 1971 copyright and its influence on possession movies, the novel has not turned into a cliché of itself. The modern author most interested in demonic possession is Michael Laimo. He writes fast-paced, suspenseful stories in which the Devil is constantly trying to enter our world. Interestingly, Joe Hill recently inserted a new twist in the demonic possession plot. In *Horns,* Hill imagines a hero who is slowly being possessed by the Devil. It is a chilling read as we are compelled to root for this hero, yet as readers, we are also frightened of him. It will be interesting to see if this critically acclaimed novel inspires other authors to explore this idea.

The next category involves satanic rituals and devil worship. These books revolve around characters who either conjure the Devil or stumble upon a demon accidentally. Either way, at some point these characters make the decision to use demonic powers to engage in evil of their own. Clive Barker, a master of the horror genre, has a knack for creating compelling tales of satanic rituals. His book *The Hellbound Heart* has terrified millions of readers and inspired the successful *Hellraiser* movie franchise. *The Hellbound Heart* is a tale of a man who, in greedily trying to summon a god of pleasure, instead unleashes the Cenobites, who are demons of torture. This backlist title is the benchmark for novels of satanic rituals and is still in print. A more recent example of the horrors caused by devil worship is *Tower Hill* by Sarah Pinborough.

The third subset is the tale of the curse or the cursed object. In these works, someone with occult powers either curses a person who has wronged him or her or, more commonly, curses an object, leaving it behind to terrorize the next person who finds it. Although many consider stories about cursed objects to belong to the subgenre that contains black magic, I feel many of them have more in common with tales of the Devil. Objects like the car in Stephen King's *Christine* are more than simply infused with evil; they are quite literally possessed by it. The demonic power is then transferred to the owner of said object, or else the curse simply destroys all who come into contact with it. Also, because it is often the innocent who find the cursed object, these stories are reminiscent of those of demonic possession.

The final plot is probably the most familiar one—tales of those who sell their souls to the Devil. This plot follows the same structure every time: the character has a wish of some sort; the Devil appears, offering all the person can desire for the price of his everlasting soul; the character debates the deal for a bit and decides that his enjoyment of his worldly life is worth the sacrifice once he dies; and, finally, the Devil comes calling for payment much earlier than the character expected. Mythologies from cultures the world over have examples of these tales. Classic literary works and operas have been built around this central conflict. And even American folklore contains well-known examples of those who have sold their souls to the Devil. It is the universal timeless appeal of getting all you could dream of for nothing (in this life at least) that keeps this story fresh. It is a cautionary tale reminding people that life is not always easy, but you need to work to gain your successes. Taking the easy way out is never a good idea, no matter how tempting; just read one of these novels to see the horrific results.

Although the story line focuses of the titles in this subgenre do vary, their appeal is fairly similar. Obviously, all the works play off our fascination with the Devil in particular and life after death in general. Our fear of demons and the action that ensues once they are unleashed are also responsible for attracting many readers to these satanic tales. In addition, these works hit on the appeal of horror as a place for readers to safely explore the darkest side of humanity. However, it is the religious aspect, either blatant or implied, that attracts the most readers. Interestingly, it is not a specific religion that is projected through these works. Rather, a more general moral tone permeates these stories. They ask us to ponder, even if only subconsciously, our own evil ways, while reaffirming our decision to stay on the right track. These stories also reinforce the hard work we do every day in order to attain our goals by illustrating that you cannot get something for nothing. It is all too easy to succumb to evil in this world, as the works in this subgenre constantly remind us, and the price of following the Devil may not be worth it.

The following list represents the best of the twenty-first century's satanic stories, with a few backlist gems that you probably already have lurking on your shelves but may have forgotten about. This list also reflects the wide range of story lines that one can find within the subgenre. You will see that most of today's biggest names in horror have gone toe-to-toe with Satan for some devilishly terrifying tales.

Barker, Clive. *The Hellbound Heart.*

Frank is bored with what life has to offer, so he tries to summon a god of pleasure. But instead he accidentally calls up demons of torture. This is a graphic work that spawned a classic horror character, Pinhead. Clive Barker set the modern standard for the demonic possession tale with this novella. *The Damnation Game* and *Everville* are also good reads in this subgenre. You probably have all three titles on your shelves, just waiting to possess a new generation of readers.

Clark, Simon. *Ghost Monster.*

Madman Justice Murrain's spirit was buried by his son, but during an archeological dig, Justice's spirit is released from its prison. He and his army of thugs return and possess the entire town in an act of revenge. This is a character-centered tale of pure evil.

Corsaro, Frank. *Kunma.*

Opera director Corsaro explores Tibetan possession mythology in this story of David, a psychiatrist who incorporates Buddhism in his practice. When the husband of one of his patients becomes possessed, David begins to learn firsthand about the Kunma, a thief of souls. This is a fast-paced, non-Christian-based possession tale.

Danielewski, Mark Z. *House of Leaves.*

With its book within a book frame, *House of Leaves* tells the story of a home under the control of the Devil through the manuscript that its former inhabitants left behind. This is a creepy, thrilling, and intelligent novel. The apprehension and unease are bolstered by the book's odd construction: footnotes, askew text, pages with only a word or two. There are real demons here, too, but it is the ones Danielewski puts in your mind as you read that are going to make you keep the lights on.

Gifune, Greg F. *Catching Hell.*

It is the summer of 1983 and four twenty-somethings take a road trip. When they make a rural pit stop off the Interstate, they encounter a town that is ruled by an evil force. The four are then thrown into a fight for their lives as their choice becomes simple: escape or die. *Catching Hell* is a tightly written, absolutely terrifying novella in the style of those you heard around the campfire as a kid.

Golden, Christopher. *Wildwood Road.*

Golden mostly writes series with established characters in the dark fantasy world, but this stand-alone horror title is a satisfying blend of the haunted house and demonic possession tales. After attending a Halloween party, a tipsy couple heads home, but when they stop to help a young girl on the side of the road, their lives are forever changed. Now the husband must find the young girl again in order to regain his wife's soul. Readers will love the chilling story and compelling protagonist.

Gran, Sara. *Come Closer.*

In this creepy novel, Amanda is a young, up-and-coming architect with a happy marriage. She is a normal woman, until she starts acting strangely. Amanda becomes promiscuous and starts stealing and being outright mean. Both Amanda and the reader are filled with dread as the unease builds and the reason for her behavior becomes devilishly clear. The prose here is unembellished, and the style is a bit more literary, but the terror is all-consuming.

Gregory, Daryl. *Pandemonium.*

This debut novel supposes an alternative reality where demonic possession is a contagious plague in which a demon possesses you for a time before moving on to a new victim. However, Del Pierce is an anomaly. He was first possessed at age 5, but now, in his 20s, the demon still lives inside him. Del has tried to keep the Hellion a secret and now wants to get rid of it once and for all. But is it too late? This fast-paced battle of good versus evil is compelling and original while still giving a nod to past horror masters.

Hill, Joe. *Horns.*

In this novel of revenge and demonic possession, Hill adds a unique twist: our hero is turning into the Devil. Ig wakes up with horns growing out of his head and has powers to see everyone's deepest and darkest thoughts. Scared of what he is becoming, Ig uses his new dark powers to get revenge for his girlfriend's murder. *Horns* is a thrilling but unsettling read, as Hill has you rooting for the Devil. We like Ig yet are completely scared of him. Talk about unsettling.

Keene, Brian. *City of the Dead.*

The king of the zombie novel imagines what would happen if the dead not only rise but do so at the behest of demons who are angry at God. This possessed zombie army, consisting of mostly animals, traps a handful of survivors in a well-stocked skyscraper and relentlessly assaults them. Keene switches the point of view among the interesting and complex survivors without losing sight of the awful bloodshed going on outside.

Kenyon, Nate. *The Reach.*

Sarah is a strange child. Her birth caused the hospital to burn down, and her grandparents can no longer handle her. Turned over to the state, Sarah lives the life of a lab rat until a young student tries to rescue her. But is Sarah worth saving? *The Reach* blends horror with psychological suspense to produce a fast-paced story that keeps you guessing.

King, Stephen. *Christine.*

Arnie Cunningham, a misfit teenager, buys a broken-down 1958 Plymouth Fury, but very soon he is obsessed with the car and possessed by its previous owner. King's classic backlist title is still chilling. *Full Dark, No Stars* also contains a very unsettling novella about cheating death with a little help from a man named Elvid for a hate-filled price.

Laimo, Michael. *Fires Rising.*

Employing an unrelentingly threatening atmosphere from the start, *Fires Rising* follows Father Anthony Pilazzo, an elderly priest in New York City, as he begins to notice strange occurrences. When his church is demolished, a dark, demonic force is unleashed. Pilazzo needs to stop the Devil from engulfing the city and all of its inhabitants. Laimo is the reigning king of this subgenre.

Lee, Edward. *The Messenger.*

The Messenger works as Lucifer's mouthpiece, and the residents of a small Florida town have become his playground. He infects them, possesses them, and makes them do his bidding. After going unchecked for years, the Messenger may finally have met his match when a mysterious man arrives. Although Lee is known for his gruesome but compelling stories, *The Messenger* is less graphic than most of his novels and may be a good entry point for new readers.

Little, Bentley. *The Town.*

When the Tomasov family moves to a small Arizona town, awful things begin happening. Gruesome deaths and strange occurrences become the norm. The townsfolk think the family is cursed, but the evil's real root may be in the Tomasovs' obscure Russian religion. This intriguing and eerie novel is infused with both chills and social satire.

Long, Jeff. *The Descent.*

If there is a historical Christ, why not a historical Satan? What if our world and Hell collided? This original horror-adventure takes these questions and leads the reader on a frightening, violent, and thought-provoking ride. *Deeper* is the sequel.

Pinborough, Sarah. *Tower Hill.*
Two criminals, one pretending to be a priest, plot to take over a small Maine town by using the power in the artifacts they have uncovered to slowly possess every resident. Two college students are wary of the new priest and lead a group that is trying to figure out what is going on. Pinborough uses an overwhelming sense of dread rather than violence to propel this tale.

Pratt, Tim, ed. *Sympathy for the Devil.*
Award-winning editor Pratt compiled this excellent collection of devilish tales from nineteenth-century classics to new, twenty-first-century stories. The stories range from humorous to unsettling to outright terrifying. Fans of Satan stories will not be disappointed.

Rollo, Gord. *Crimson.*
A group of boys stumbles upon the possessed remains of a murdered family buried in a well. The demon tempts the boys to help him, but they manage to resist. Ten years later, the demon has escaped and goes on a murderous rampage. He is still angry with the boys and tries to frame one of them for the murders. *Crimson* can be gruesome at times, but with its small-town setting and adolescent protagonists hiding a secret, it is a great read-alike for fans of Stephen King or Peter Straub.

Saul, John. *The Devil's Labyrinth.*
Ryan's father has died in Iraq, and Ryan has become the target of school bullies, so his mom sends him to Catholic school, hoping he can have a fresh start. But the school is not a safe haven. A rogue priest, who has learned to use his exorcism powers to control the evil inside everyone, is testing his power on the students with gruesome results. This is an edge-of-your-seat, bloody ride, with a current events angle.

BECKY'S DEVIL PICKS

Fires Rising, by Michael Laimo

Horns, by Joe Hill

The Reach, by Nate Kenyon

TITLE/AUTHOR LIST

Catching Hell, by Greg F. Gifune

Christine, by Stephen King

City of the Dead, by Brian Keene

Come Closer, by Sara Gran

Crimson, by Gord Rollo

The Damnation Game, by Clive Barker

Deeper, by Jeff Long

The Descent, by Jeff Long

The Devil's Labyrinth, by John Saul

Everville, by Clive Barker

The Exorcist, by William Peter Blatty

Fires Rising, by Michael Laimo

Full Dark, No Stars, by Stephen King

Ghost Monster, by Simon Clark

The Hellbound Heart, by Clive Barker

Horns, by Joe Hill

House of Leaves, by Mark Z. Danielewski

Kunma, by Frank Corsaro

The Messenger, by Edward Lee

Pandemonium, by Daryl Gregory

The Reach, by Nate Kenyon

Sympathy for the Devil, edited by Tim Pratt

Tower Hill, by Sarah Pinborough

The Town, by Bentley Little

Wildwood Road, by Christopher Golden

12

COMIC HORROR
Laughing in the Face of Fear

Having spent the last eleven chapters focusing on the fact that horror is all about provoking terror, it is now time to switch gears and highlight an important subgenre: comic horror. What is so funny about zombies, vampires, and vicious monsters? Plenty. Horror has many conventions and motifs that are used throughout the genre. These are tried-and-true tricks of the trade that are sure to create unsettling atmospheres, frightening situations, and terrified readers. Among the most common are the isolated setting, the troubled, down-on-his-luck protagonist, and the angry spirit out for revenge. The comic horror novel takes these go-to situations and parodies them to create both chills and laughs.

In movies the horror parody has been quite popular. The *Scream* movie franchise is a great example of comic horror.[1] Directed by horror movie legend Wes Craven, these films parody the genre with a knowing wink and nod. More recently, *Shaun of the Dead* took the zombie craze in a new direction by mixing equal parts shambling monsters and straight-up laughs.[2] These comic horror films and others like them are a big hit with audiences, so it should come as no surprise that horror novelists have been turning to the subgenre in droves.

The benchmark author for all comic horror books is Christopher Moore. He reliably writes funny, thought-provoking, and chilling novels that satirize both the horror genre and the human condition. In *You Suck*, two young vampires need to learn how to feed and love in modern California. Another long-standing comic horror author is Mario Acevedo; however, his books tend to range toward the sillier side of the subgenre.

The comic horror novel had been slowly gaining in popularity since the release of *Scream*, but in 2009 it exploded when Quirk Books took the subgenre to a whole new level by releasing *Pride and Prejudice and Zombies* by Seth Grahame-Smith. Grahame-Smith took about 80 percent of the public domain text of Austen's classic and inserted zombies and zombie hunters. The ensuing novel was a huge best seller and spawned an entirely new subgenre of literature called "the mash-up." Quirk and other publishers have since put out numerous horror mash-ups of literary classics.

So it seems comic horror is here to stay. The review sources are regularly highlighting this new subgenre. In fact, many of the titles in this list have received starred reviews. But why are these novels such a hit with reviewers and fans? Their main draw lies in satire. The comic horror novel is most enjoyed by the true horror fan. Someone who regularly reads the horror authors and titles found in the previous chapters and appreciates the genre's tropes will crave these books that, with a knowing wink and nod, poke fun at horror while still respecting it. The humor is born out of horror's past and is built on the foundation laid out in the preceding lists. Comic horror fans love this insider's feel to the stories. They are part of an exclusive club who "get" the jokes, references, and puns. Good comic horror, like the books on this "sure bets" list, will seamlessly blend chills and satire, allowing readers to be scared and have a good laugh, both at the same time.

Acevedo, Mario. *The Nymphos of Rocky Flats.*
In this, the first of the popular Felix Gomez series, Acevedo introduces Gomez, an ex-U.S. soldier turned vampire, who is hired to investigate an outbreak of nymphomania among female guards at a plant. Gomez's investigation reveals a government cover-up, vampire hunters, a dryad, and some aliens. Readers should expect action, feelings of panic and terror, and a satisfyingly satirical tone with each of the books in this series.

Anderson, Kevin David. *Night of the Living Trekkies.*
At a science fiction fan convention, a virus begins to spread. Soon a small band of strangers is forced to work together to find a way to escape an all-out attack by zombies hungry for live flesh. A combination of dead-on parody, *Star Trek* trivia, and hilarious dialogue make this original comic novel a fan and critic favorite.

Anderson, Kevin J., ed. *Blood Lite: An Anthology of Humorous Horror Stories Presented by the Horror Writers Association.*
Helped along by the popularity of contributor Charlaine Harris, Anderson's compilation of comic horror was a surprise best seller.

This anthology gathers works both funny and frightening written by members of the Horror Writers Association. Second and third editions have since followed, illustrating comic horror's foothold with writers and readers.

Becker, Robin M. *Brains: A Zombie Memoir.*

A virus outbreak turns millions of people into zombies. As the survivors begin a war against the zombies, one zombie, former professor Jack Barnes, who has retained his brain function, sets off to find the virus's creator, stop the war, and hopefully gain equal rights for zombies. This fake memoir is both intelligent and humorous. It is a great suggestion for readers caught up in the current zombie craze.

Browne, S. G. *Breathers: A Zombie's Lament.*

This romantic zombie comedy opens in the middle of the story. Andy is lying on the floor of his kitchen staring at a refrigerator packed with the chopped-up parts of his parents. Andy takes the reader back to explain how he became a zombie and how he just wants to be accepted for who he is. However, Andy's attempts to gain equal rights for zombies hilariously backfire as he and his zombie friends begin to realize their true natures. Although the laughs quickly stack up throughout the novel, the ending is as chilling as any horror novel included in this book.

Burrow, B. J. *The Changed.*

The dead begin rising all over the world, but they are nothing like George Romero warned us about. Because they are sentient and only eat humans who are brain damaged, "the changed," as they call themselves, begin to question why the government can kill them at will. One of the changed, Christian, decides to fight for zombie rights and runs for senator. Humorous appearances by pop culture figures, including Elmo, both add to the chuckles and reinforce the chilling realism of this ultimately horrific story.

Cooper, Seamus. *The Mall of Cthulhu.*

Ted thought he was done battling evil after he destroyed a nest of vampires back in college, but when he finds a group of Lovecraft enthusiasts intent on raising the author's greatest monsters, Ted and his friend Laura must save the suburbs from the evil of the Necronomicon. Whether you are a diehard Lovecraft fan or not, this is silly horror at its best; the monsters are evil and social commentary is relentless.

Egolf, Tristan. *Kornwolf.*

Ephraim is your typical Amish boy—that is, until the moon is full. Then he turns into a bloodthirsty werewolf, with an uncanny resemblance to Richard Nixon. Cynical reporter Owen begins to exploit the rumors of a werewolf to further his own career. However, when the werewolf turns out to be real, the town may be in for a bloody Halloween. Very few escape ridicule in Egolf's creepy tale of the grotesque.

Fox, Andrew. *Fat White Vampire Blues.*

Jules, a 350-pound, taxi-cab-driving vampire, is confronted by a new black vampire, Malice X, who is intent on making Jules's life a living hell. Jules, a newish vampire himself, enlists the help of his maker and a vampire friend in an attempt to stand up to Malice X's bullying. Jules is a hapless hero, whom readers will grow to love. Fox combines hysterical situations with horrific events to produce satisfying results. Jules returns in *Bride of the Fat White Vampire.*

Geillor, Harrison. *The Zombies of Lake Woebegotten.*

In this parody of Garrison Keillor's portrayal of Minnesotans as stead-fast people who don't want to draw attention to themselves, the dead (both human and animal) begin to rise as zombies. The good people of Lake Woebegotten must band together to save themselves. However, one resident, Mr. Leavitt, is a secret serial killer, who tries to reanimate his victims and create his own zombie army. Geillor's inventive novel is both an obvious satire and a chilling story of the monsters that lurk among us.

Goldsher, Alan. *Paul Is Undead: The British Zombie Invasion.*

The British Invasion is presented in an alternate universe where John, Paul, and George are zombies being controlled by Ringo, who is actu-ally a ninja lord. The story roughly follows the real career of the Beatles but with bloody and funny results. Horror and music fans alike will love this clever novel.

Grahame-Smith, Seth, and Jane Austen. *Pride and Prejudice and Zombies: The Classic Regency Romance—Now with Ultraviolent Zombie Mayhem.*

Take equal parts Regency manners and zombie mayhem, mix them together, and you get an England overrun by "unmentionables." This mash-up works because Grahame-Smith strategically inserts the zom-bies without changing the overall story much. In fact, the zombies answer many key questions in the original, such as why Charlotte marries Mr. Collins. Elizabeth and Darcy are both well-trained zombie assassins who must kill zombies as they move toward their happily ever after. A prequel, *Dawn of the Dreadfuls* by Steve Hockensmith, is also available.

Harris, Charlaine, and Toni L. P. Kelner, eds. *Death's Excellent Vacation.*
Ever wonder what happens when supernatural beings go on vacation? Harris and Kelner have. They enlisted their fellow paranormal and horror authors to help in this amusing and original collection. Although some of the stories in this collection move toward the paranormal, several stories, such as those by Jeff Abbott, Christopher Golden, and Chris Grabenstein, are 100 percent horror. Fans of this subgenre will not want to miss these stories.

Langford, David. *Different Kinds of Darkness.*
In each of these thirty-six fantasy, science fiction, and horror stories, Langford plays with genre conventions. Fans of any of these genres will enjoy reading about their favorite situations and clichés in an amusing and outright strange light. These are reprints of stories that were originally written between 1975 and 2003.

Martinez, A. Lee. *Gil's All Fright Diner.*
Earl, a vampire, and Duke, a werewolf, stop in the middle of the desert to grab a bite to eat at Gil's Diner. While visiting, the pair helps the owner stop a zombie attack. The two stay on in the small town to help solve other amusing paranormal problems. This novel is a fast-paced, unpredictable romp that has more substance than you might think.

Moore, Christopher. *A Dirty Job.*
When Charlie's wife dies right after giving birth, he swears that a tall man in a green suit was standing over her as she died. When strangers begin dropping dead in front of him, Charlie has had enough and goes in search of answers. Turns out he is a Death Merchant who must gather up souls in order to save them. But can he be a good father if he keeps killing people? This poignant and comical story leads to a final confrontation with Death himself.

Pendle, George. *Death: A Life.*
Death narrates his autobiography in this amazing novel. He begins his story just before Earth is created, but it takes him awhile to find his calling. But being death is stressful, and he tries a bit of "life" on the

side. These experiments lead to an addiction that could kill him. How will he recover? This is a wickedly funny, original, and tender portrait of a great villain. *Death: A Life* is black humor at its finest.

Strand, Jeff. *Benjamin's Parasite.*

After attending the funeral of a student who went on a murderous rampage with a meat cleaver, Benjamin starts to feel odd. At first, he has strange cravings, but then he gets intense stomach pains. Turns out he has an intestinal parasite, but before he can have it removed, Benjamin is kidnapped by a bounty hunter. As if things couldn't get any worse, or any crazier, Benjamin thinks the parasite is trying to talk to him. Strand deftly balances both comedy and horror in this fast-paced tale.

Wong, David. *John Dies at the End.*

David and John try a drug called "soy sauce" that seems cool and psychedelic, until they realize they are not hallucinating. The drug has actually opened up a portal to Hell that allows a number of murderous monsters to break free. John and David have to stop them from destroying the world. *John Dies at the End* is a horrifying spoof that will have you alternately smiling and cringing.

BECKY'S COMIC PICKS

Blood Lite, edited by Kevin J. Anderson

Breathers: A Zombie's Lament, by S. G. Browne

A Dirty Job, by Christopher Moore

NOTES

1. For more information about each of the *Scream* films, go to the Internet Movie Database, www.imdb.com/title/tt0117571/ (accessed November 30, 2010).
2. For more information about *Shaun of the Dead,* go to the Internet Movie Database, www.imdb.com/title/tt0365748/ (accessed November 30, 2010).

TITLE/AUTHOR LIST

Benjamin's Parasite, by Jeff Strand

Blood Lite: An Anthology of Humorous Horror Stories Presented by the Horror Writers Association, edited by Kevin J. Anderson

Brains: A Zombie Memoir, by Robin M. Becker

Breathers: A Zombie's Lament, by S. G. Browne

Bride of the Fat White Vampire, by Andrew Fox

The Changed, by B. J. Burrow

Dawn of the Dreadfuls, by Steve Hockensmith

Death: A Life, by George Pendle

Death's Excellent Vacation, edited by Charlaine Harris and Toni L. P. Kelner

Different Kinds of Darkness, by David Langford

A Dirty Job, by Christopher Moore

Fat White Vampire Blues, by Andrew Fox

Gil's All Fright Diner, by A. Lee Martinez

John Dies at the End, by David Wong

Kornwolf, by Tristan Egolf

The Mall of Cthulhu, by Seamus Cooper

Night of the Living Trekkies, by Kevin David Anderson

The Nymphos of Rocky Flats, by Mario Acevedo

Paul Is Undead: The British Zombie Invasion, by Alan Goldsher

Pride and Prejudice and Zombies: The Classic Regency Romance—Now with Ultraviolent Zombie Mayhem, by Seth Grahame-Smith and Jane Austen

You Suck: A Love Story, by Christopher Moore

The Zombies of Lake Woebegotten, by Harrison Geillor

13

MOVING BEYOND THE HAUNTED HOUSE
Whole Collection Options for Horror Readers

Although librarians spend much time creating genre boundaries, the fact of the matter is that readers' tastes do not fit neatly into the genre boxes we have defined. In fact, though readers may prefer one genre over another, in reality, they read all over the map. Horror readers are no different from any other type of reader. In fact, in many ways, horror readers are more willing to move outside their favorite genre for their leisure reading. With so many horror elements creeping into all types of fiction, your library's entire collection is a bounty for horror fans. You just need to know in which direction to steer them. This chapter addresses your library's entire collection and identifies genres, formats, and specific titles for you to suggest to your horror patrons. Specifically it covers psychological suspense, dark fantasy, supernatural thrillers, nonfiction, graphic novels, audiobooks, short stories, and film.

WHOLE COLLECTION READERS' ADVISORY

The term "whole collection readers' advisory" was first coined by Neal Wyatt in an article in *Library Journal* back in 2006:

> Whole collection RA recognizes that our collections are richer than a short list of similar titles and that the world of the book is often more complex than the traditional list of three to five suggestions we generally make. Sometimes we don't want a read-alike because it removes us from the internal world of the book we loved. We are fascinated with a particular aspect of the title in hand and want that reading experience to be extended.[1]

The idea of whole collection RA has gained traction since 2006, and now librarians are trying to consider the entirety of their holdings when making suggestions to readers. Horror readers are ripe to try different genres and formats. They are adventurous readers who tend to not mind sex or violence in their stories. They enjoy speculative elements and a steadily building pace. But most of all, they like the emotional pull of a story. They want to experience the dark feelings of anxiety, dread, and terror when they read.

Although horror readers may browse all the books you have labeled with a horror sticker, there is so much more waiting for them to enjoy in your stacks. As an RA librarian, it is your job to remind them of the breadth of your holdings, pointing them to titles and authors they would just love if only they knew where to look for them. In this chapter I will review the main appeal factors of some of these whole collection options as they specifically pertain to horror readers. Before I begin though, I need to make a few clarifications. These suggestions are not horror. They will not be exactly the same as a horror read, but they may be just the thing for a horror reader in a rut. Also, the lists of suggestions I have provided throughout this chapter are not meant to be taken as the best or only choices in their categories. I have made an effort to provide a mix of titles. These are books that span the wide appeal of each of these genres or formats, providing you with lists you can actually use as you help your patrons.

PSYCHOLOGICAL SUSPENSE

Probably the closest you can get to horror these days without entering the genre's city limits are the books loosely classified as psychological suspense. Slowly gaining legitimacy as its own genre, psychological suspense refers to books that, like horror, put the uneasy atmosphere in the forefront. The difference here is the absence of the supernatural element. The monsters in psychological suspense are flesh-and-blood individuals who are frighteningly real, not unearthly in any sense. These are books filled with serial killers, stalkers, and evil masterminds. They play with the psyches of their victims and their readers. Tension in these novels builds, the atmosphere is nightmarish, the chills do not let up, and the plot resolutions are disturbing and unclear. These are fairly literary novels filled with darkness, plot twists, and obsession. The experience of reading a psychological suspense novel is one of confusion, unsettledness, and anxiety—all a perfect fit for horror readers. If you want to understand the genre, try one of the two classic purveyors of psychological suspense: an Alfred Hitchcock movie or a Patricia Highsmith novel. Box 13.1 also provides a list of ten sure-bet psychological suspense authors accompanied by a suggested starting title for each.

Box 13.1   *10 Psychological Suspense Picks for Horror Readers*

Peter Abrahams, *End of Story*

Alden Bell, *The Reapers Are the Angels*

Dan Chaon, *Await Your Reply*

Gillian Flynn, *Dark Places*

Henry James, *The Turn of the Screw and Other Stories*

Jeff Lindsay, *Darkly Dreaming Dexter*

Joyce Carol Oates, *Zombie*

Ruth Rendell, *13 Steps Down*

Scott Smith, *A Simple Plan*

Sarah Waters, *The Little Stranger*

DARK FANTASY

Many horror readers love the darkness and unexplainable elements in horror but want a break from the extreme tension and anxiety. Dark fantasy, with its sinister brand of magic, is a great option here. Some of these authors use traditional horror creatures in less terrifying ways, while others simply create a magical world to look at the dark side of humanity. The big difference between dark fantasy and horror is that dark fantasy's main goal is not to produce feelings of outright terror in the reader; rather, it is to create a dark world where bad things can and do happen. However, while horror and psychological suspense are extremely dark and unsettling, dark fantasy encompasses a wide range of tone and mood. Some novels add a touch of mystery, others mythology, and still others, some romance. As a result, dark fantasy appeals to a wide range of readers. The reigning king of the genre in all age levels is undoubtedly Neil Gaiman, whose books serve as the perfect starting point for anyone who wants to understand the genre. Box 13.2 features ten authors and titles to get you started.

Box 13.2   *10 Dark Fantasy Picks for Horror Readers*

Kelley Armstrong, Women of the Otherworld series (begins with *Bitten*).

Emma Bull, *War for the Oaks*

Jim Butcher, The Dresden Files series (begins with *Storm Front*)

Jonathan Carroll, *The Land of Laughs*

Raymond Feist, *Faerie Tale*

Neil Gaiman, *Neverwhere*

Jim Knipfel, *These Children Who Come at You with Knives*

China Miéville, *The City and the City*

Audrey Niffenegger, *Her Fearful Symmetry*

Jeff VanderMeer, *Finch*

SUPERNATURAL THRILLER

As I have mentioned numerous times throughout this text, horror elements have been creeping into just about every genre of popular fiction. Nowhere is this shift more obvious than in the emergence of the extremely popular supernatural thriller. This subgenre of the thriller began as traditional horror novelists started branching out and exploring more adrenaline-based story lines in which the pacing and investigative elements began to supersede the uneasy atmosphere in importance. Horror authors like Dean Koontz, F. Paul Wilson, and Jonathan Maberry have best-selling supernatural thriller series that feature a fast-paced story with otherworldly elements. However, the supernatural thriller has taken on a life of its own, and now authors like Douglas Preston and Lincoln Child have fashioned best-selling careers by providing readers with books filled with unrelenting action, in which brave heroes fight a supernatural evil out to take over the world. Other popular supernatural thriller story lines are typified by Charlie Huston's Joe Pitt series in which a common horror trope (in this case the vampire) is used as a backdrop for what is essentially an investigative crime story. No matter the details, the supernatural thriller differs from traditional horror in its focus. While horror puts atmosphere at the forefront for its story, the supernatural thriller is all about the adrenaline rush of the fast-paced action. These are dark stories with scary supernatural beings, but they focus on the heroes and action rather than the terror. An investigative element is also prominent in the supernatural thriller. Box 13.3 offers ten authors and titles that represent a range of what the supernatural thriller has to offer.

Box 13.3   *10 Supernatural Thriller Picks for Horror Readers*

Michael Crichton, *Prey*

Guillermo del Toro and Chuck Hogan, the Strain series (begins with *The Strain*)

Mira Grant, the Newsflesh series (begins with *Feed*)

Daniel Hecht, Cree Black series (begins with *City of Masks*)

Charlie Huston, Joe Pitt series (begins with *Already Dead*)

Robert Masello, *Blood and Ice*

David Morrell, *Creepers*

Tom Piccirilli, *The Midnight Road*

Douglas Preston and Lincoln Child, Pendergast novels (begin with *Relic*)

James Rollins, *Amazonia*

NONFICTION

Believe it or not, horror nonfiction has always had a big following. From true tales of real ghosts to encyclopedias of scary creatures and from biographies of horror masters to true crime, there are many treasures for the horror fiction reader to find in the nonfiction stacks. The most popular nonfiction horror titles in the public library are generally the books about the haunted areas in your community. Remember, in chapter 2, I mentioned that many readers like horror because it validates their belief in the supernatural. These books hit that appeal directly on the head. In the list in box 13.4, I have offered a national version of one of these titles, but you should make sure your library has the local equivalent. The other nonfiction area popular with horror fans is the true crime section. Just as serial-killer fiction can be appealing to horror fans who do not mind flesh-and-blood monsters in their books, true crime works as well because it is the nonfiction equivalent. I have included a book by Ann Rule, the queen of true crime, but really, all you need to do is lead a horror reader who seems interested in true crime to that section of the stacks and let her browse for herself.

The newly emerging area in horror nonfiction is the encyclopedia of horror characters. Publishers are putting out 400-plus-page "reference" books on everything from vampires to werewolves to fairies, at all reading levels. Recently, another new nonfiction trend has begun emerging with the "survival guide." In box 13.4, I suggest the book by Max Brooks that began the trend; however, you can now find a guide on how to survive just about any supernatural attack. Other popular nonfiction options include biographies and books about horror literature and films. Box 13.4 offers a list of ten nonfiction titles to offer to your horror readers.

Box 13.4 *10 Nonfiction Picks for Horror Readers*

Max Brooks, *The Zombie Survival Guide*

John Michael Greer, *The New Encyclopedia of the Occult*

Rosemary Guiley, *The Encyclopedia of Vampires, Werewolves, and Other Monsters*

Stephen King, *Danse Macabre*

Jonathan Maberry and David F. Kramer, *The Cryptopedia: A Dictionary of the Weird, Strange, and Downright Bizarre*

Carol K. Mack, *A Field Guide to Demons, Fairies, Fallen Angels, and Other Subversive Spirits*

J. Gordon Melton, *The Vampire Book: The Encyclopedia of the Undead*

Michael Norman and Beth Scott, *Haunted America*

Kim Paffenroth, *Gospel of the Living Dead: George Romero's Visions of Hell on Earth*

Ann Rule, *The Stranger beside Me*

OTHER FORMATS

Although the preceding genres are a great place to lead horror readers who are looking for something new, it is also important to remember that there are many horror options in formats other than the traditional printed novel. Sometimes patrons need to be reminded that horror comes in all shapes and sizes and that those different formats are still in the library. They just may be on a different shelf or in a different department. Following are some categories of horror materials that you can find in your library—the only difference is that they are not in the traditional novel format.

Graphic Novels

Horror readers tend to enjoy graphic novels because of the horror novel's focus on description and adjectives. As mentioned in chapter 2, a good horror novel allows the reader to feel the action and the fear with all five senses. The graphic novel's use of illustrations to help tell its story adds a new element to this appeal. However, the range of graphic novels available is so vast that there are literally hundreds of titles in every genre, which may satisfy your horror readers. In an attempt to get you started, I have offered ten series and titles in box 13.5. I have included a range from dark fantasy to science fiction and from paranormal to pure horror. These are new and old titles, but all can be easily found in most public library adult graphic novel collections. When helping readers to select the right graphic novel for them, make sure they open the book and look at the drawings first. Readers need to be comfortable with the artist's style, the level of gore depicted, and how the story is laid out as much as they need to be interested in the story itself. For more information on helping graphic novel readers, try *The Readers' Advisory Guide to Graphic Novels* (ALA Editions, 2010) by Francisca Goldsmith, and for more horror graphic novel title suggestions, try Michael Pawuk's *Graphic Novels: A Genre Guide to Comic Books, Manga, and More* (Libraries Unlimited, 2007).

Box 13.5   *10 Graphic Novel Picks for Horror Readers*

Neil Gaiman, Sandman series (begins with *Preludes and Nocturnes*)

Joe Hill, Locke and Key series (begins with *Welcome to Lovecraft*)

Robert Kirkman, The Walking Dead series (begins with *The Walking Dead: Compendium One*)

John Layman, Marvel Zombies vs. Army of Darkness series

Mike Mignola, Hellboy series (begins with *Hellboy: Seed of Destruction*)

Alan Moore, Swamp Thing series (begins with *Saga of the Swamp Thing*)

Steve Niles, *30 Days of Night*

Scott Snyder and Stephen King, American Vampire series (begins with *American Vampire*)

Ben Templesmith, Wormwood: Gentleman Corpse series (begins with *Wormwood: Birds, Bees, Blood, and Booze*)

Brian K. Vaughan, Y: The Last Man series (begins with *Y: The Last Man; Unmanned*)

Audiobooks

Many people are first introduced to horror stories around a campfire. Chances are you probably heard a horror story before you ever read one. Also, back in the days of radio, horror-based programming was extremely popular. Add to the mix an overall rise in interest in audiobooks, and suggesting a horror title on audio is a great option for your horror fans. Although not every one of their favorite authors will appear in audio, in box 13.6, I have offered ten titles that offer a range of pleasures. It is important to note that the newer titles on the list have all been nominated for an Audie, the award given annually to the best audiobook by the Audio Publishers Association. Specifically, I have included a title by Scott Sigler to remind you that he releases all his novels as free podcasts before they are printed and distributed in book form. He is an author who has embraced the oral tradition. As a result, his work stands out in this format.

Box 13.6   *10 Audiobook Picks for Horror Readers*

Max Brooks, *World War Z: An Oral History of the Zombie War*

Classic Radio Horror, *Horror in the Air: Radio Tales of Terror,*
    Weirdness and the Occult

Keith Donohue, *The Stolen Child*

Neil Gaiman, *The Graveyard Book*

Leopoldo Gout, *Ghost Radio*

Stephen King, *The Mist*

Edgar Allan Poe, *Edgar Allan Poe Audio Collection*

Douglas Preston and Lincoln Child, *Brimstone*

Scott Sigler, *Infected*

Dan Simmons, *Drood*

Short Story Collections

Horror is alive and well in the short story format. Horror readers seek out short stories not only to enjoy their favorite established authors but also to identify new voices. It is a format popular with many horror fans and should not be overlooked when working with readers.

The most important advice for the readers' advisor who is helping readers with horror story collections is to become familiar with the top editors in the industry. Considered the best editor in the horror community, Ellen Datlow is without peer. Her annual collection, *The Best Horror of the Year,* is a must purchase for any library with horror readers. She edits at least two other collections every year. Because of her proven skill as an editor, her calls for submissions attract the best horror writers in the world. Another editor on the rise is Lisa Morton. Both women are represented in box 13.7.

The list in box 13.7 is focused on acclaimed collections containing horror short stories of which you should be aware. Many of the titles listed have become so popular that they have turned into series, with new stories year after year. These suggestions, which do not include those story collections that were mentioned in previous subgenre lists, are worth your attention. One, *Tales of the Cthulhu Mythos,* is interesting because it includes some of the best stories by H. P. Lovecraft along with many newer stories by modern authors who have been inspired by the horror legend. In general, story collections of tales inspired by Lovecraft are popular with readers.

One practical note: collections can be hard to find in the stacks because they are scattered around. Of course, collections by a single author will be easy to locate next to his or her other works, but other collections demand that RA librarians remember them, use them in displays, and otherwise incorporate them in their work.

Box 13.7   *10 Short Story Collections for Horror Readers*

Christopher Conlon, ed., *He Is Legend: An Anthology Celebrating Richard Matheson*

Ellen Datlow, ed., *Inferno: New Tales of the Supernatural*

Neil Gaiman and Al Sarrantonio, eds., *Stories: All-New Tales*

Del Howison and Jeff Gelb, eds., Dark Delicacies series (begins with *Dark Delicacies*)

John Langan, *Mr. Gaunt and Other Uneasy Encounters*

Joe Lansdale, ed., Retro Pulp Tales series (begins with *Retro Pulp Tales*)

H. P. Lovecraft, *Tales of the Cthulhu Mythos*

Lisa Morton, ed., *Midnight Walk: 14 Original Stories of Terror and Suspense*

Peter Straub, ed., *Poe's Children: The New Horror; An Anthology*

Douglas E. Winter, ed., *Prime Evil: New Stories by the Masters of Modern Horror*

Horror Films and Television Series

Horror films and television shows have a long history of capturing our imagination. Like graphic novels, this visual version of horror storytelling takes the genre and adds to it. As the horror story unfolds on the screen, many factors enhance its visceral nature and ratchet up the fear. The director can manipulate shots and add eerie music, adding new elements of terror above and beyond what our own mind creates while we are alone reading a horror novel. In box 13.8, I have proposed a list of ten films that, in my experience, appeal to horror fiction fans. Some are based on horror books, while others are simply considered among the best the genre has to offer. Think of this list as a starting point, but for those readers who want more, you will need to consult a specific reference book on horror films.[2]

Box 13.8 *10 Horror Films for Horror Readers*

The Blair Witch Project	The Last Man on Earth
Dracula	Night of the Living Dead
The Exorcist	The Ring
Halloween	Rosemary's Baby
Jaws	The Shining

The same should be said when offering television suggestions to horror fans. In box 13.9, I have proposed a list of ten television series that would most appeal to horror readers. All are readily available on DVD through your regular ILL channels. This list was compiled from various "best" lists, from horror-focused, Internet resources, and from my own experience working with horror fans, but I also suggest regularly checking the Syfy channel.[3] This is the most consistently horror-friendly television station. The point here is that the readers' advisor must at least consider horror film and television suggestions when working with horror readers.

Box 13.9 *10 Horror Television Series for Horror Readers*

Buffy the Vampire Slayer	Tales from the Crypt
Dexter	Tales from the Darkside
The Hitchhiker	The Twilight Zone
Masters of Horror	Twin Peaks
Rod Serling's Night Gallery	The Walking Dead

NOTES

1. Neal Wyatt, "Redefining RA: Reading Maps Remake RA," *Library Journal* (November 11, 2006), www.libraryjournal.com/article/CA6383011.html #Whole%20Collection%20RA.

2. One of the best reviewed and most public library appropriate horror film titles is David Skal, *The Monster Show: A Cultural History of Horror* (New York: W. W. Norton, 1993). To search your local collection, use the subject heading Horror films—History and Criticism.

3. "Top 10 Greatest Horror TV Shows of All Time," Esplatter: The Independent Source for Horror, www.esplatter.com/news.php?id=706 (accessed February 9, 2011); "Best Horror TV Series with at Least 1,000 Votes," IMDB, www.imdb.com/ search/title?genres=horror&title_type=tv_series&num_votes=1000,&sort=user _rating,desc (accessed February 9, 2011); "Top 5 Horror Television Shows," *Scary Film Review,* http://scaryfilm.blogspot.com/2011/01/top-5-horror-television -shows.html (accessed February 9, 2011); the Syfy channel's program schedule and more can be accessed at www.syfy.com.

14

SOWING THE SEEDS OF FEAR
Horror Resources and Marketing

Armed with a full collection of horror authors and titles to suggest, as well as some whole collection options, you are now ready for the final pieces of the horror readers' advisory puzzle: resources, collection development, and marketing. This chapter will focus on where you can go to find new and more detailed information about horror fiction, how to evaluate and build your horror collections, and, finally, how to get the word out to your horror-craving patrons.

HORROR RESOURCES

One of the most common misconceptions that plague librarians who help leisure readers, especially genre-loving readers, is that they must have read a book in order to suggest it. In reality, this requirement would be analogous to forcing a reference librarian to read the entire encyclopedia from cover to cover before she could ever answer a question. Just as the reference librarian turns to specific books or websites to assist patrons, the readers' advisor can also choose from a wide range of reference sources to fill in the gaps in her personal knowledge and help her patron find his next good read; it is simply a matter of knowing where to begin. In this section, I will highlight the best horror resources for librarians. These are the tools you can trust to provide you with information that is directly targeted to your audience—the horror patron. I will list my favorite book, web, and database resources for horror information and offer tips on how to best organize and monitor these resources.

Becky's Book Picks

Too often, today's librarians run straight to the computer when asked to help a reader find a book to read. We often forget the wonderful print resources that are available. Besides this text, I have a few other horror print resources that I refer to frequently:

If you are looking for lists of more horror titles by subgenre, turn to *Hooked on Horror III: A Guide to Reading Interests* by Anthony Fonseca and June Michelle Pulliam.

For horror suggestions based on their appeal, without concern for their subgenre, the same authors also have *Read On . . . Horror Fiction.*

If you want to keep up with the best of new horror from all over the world, from every print outlet, traditional and electronic, including an annual essay on the current state of horror, look no farther than Ellen Datlow's annual Best Horror of the Year series.[1] This new series continues the work Datlow did for many years as the editor of The Year's Best Fantasy and Horror series.[2] By letting horror star in its own "best" series, Datlow has been able to raise the genre's profile and bring attention to more authors and publishers. This series is a must-have for any library with a horror collection. In fact, if you are reading this book, you have enough horror patrons to justify purchasing Datlow's compilation on an annual basis.

If you are looking for books in which horror writers talk about why they love the genre and give their opinions on what you should be reading, try Stephen King's *Danse Macabre* and Matthew Warner's *Horror Isn't a 4-Letter Word: Essays on Writing and Appreciating the Genre.* Both books will give you and your horror fans an intimate peek into the genre.

Becky's Web Picks

The Internet is filled with resources for horror fans, but the list of those resources that are most helpful to librarians is a bit smaller. Here are the free web resources I most rely on in alphabetical order:

Dark Scribe Magazine (www.darkscribemagazine.com) is an online magazine about "the books that keep you up at night." Although not exclusively about horror, horror is its main focus. The magazine contains dark fiction reviews, author interviews, articles, and essays, and the editors also give out Black Quill Awards annually.

The Horror Fiction Review (http://thehorrorfictionreview.blogspot .com/) is a thoughtful, well-organized site. It offers horror reviews for fans of horror fiction, by fans of horror fiction; thus, the editors warn, you will find that the reviews which make it into the monthly updates are generally positive. *The Horror Fiction Review* began in 2003 as a printed fanzine, but it has been online since 2008. The site also runs interviews with horror authors.

Horror World (www.horrorworld.org) is the best of the "horror community" websites out there. It compiles reviews and author interviews as well as producing its own newsletter and podcast. There are pages with further horror links, charts allowing access to free horror e-book downloads, and message boards on various topics. This is the best place to find horror fans, authors, and publishers gathering online to discuss the genre.

The Horror Writers Association (HWA; www.horror.org) maintains a web page chock full of information for horror readers. Most notably, HWA gives out the most prestigious award in horror, the Bram Stoker Award. Recently, the association created a membership level for fans, making it easier for anyone who enjoys horror to join.

Monster Librarian (www.monsterlibrarian.com) provides book reviews, author interviews, lists of suggested horror reading at every age level, and librarian-specific horror resources. Monster Librarian also frequently teams up with some of the other sites mentioned here to draw attention to new horror titles.

RA for All: Horror (http://raforallhorror.blogspot.com) is the website and blog I maintain to discuss horror news, issues, and resources as well as provide free updates to this book. It is an easily searchable and accessible repository for librarian-specific information about horror fiction, including reviews, annotated reading lists, and a comprehensive list of horror resources.

Many horror fans blog about horror. Thankfully, the most conscientious of these bloggers have banded together to form the *Horror Blogger*

Alliance, creating an online home for the horror blogger community (http://horrorbloggeralliance.blogspot.com). The home page provides access to every blog in the alliance as well as listing any news in the horror community.

Becky's Database Pick

On the fee-based end of the online resource spectrum, I find the horror information in the leisure reading database NoveList to be extremely helpful.[3] NoveList has recently updated its interface, beefed up its horror content, and added valuable appeal-based searching. For example, figure 14.1 is a picture of the main page of NoveList with the recommended Reading Lists for horror highlighted. A simple click on one of these links will bring you to an updated, annotated list of newer horror materials that fit into the listed categories. Figure 14.2 is a screen shot of the author description for Jonathan Maberry. These author descriptions focus on what is most appealing about the author and include Start With title options. Please notice the read-alike suggestions provided to the right of the author description. Any title or series entries will also have appropriate read-alike suggestions. NoveList's commitment to the horror reader shows in its content. Those with access to this rich database should remember to consult it when helping horror fans.

Figure 14.1 *NoveList—Horror Lists*

Final Resource Tip

Although these are the horror resources that I have found to be the most helpful and the most reliable, I am aware that trying to provide a list of resources in the twenty-first century can be problematic, especially when we are talking about free, web-based resources. The problem is twofold. First, there are literally thousands of websites that cover horror from one angle or another. It is very difficult both to figure out which sites are most worth your time and to keep track of the ones you do find helpful. Second, web resources that you come to rely on can disappear forever, without a moment's notice. As a result, any discussion of resources today must include advice on how to manage those resources.

Once you identify the resources that you find the most helpful, you must find a way to keep track of them. My favorite online tool for managing, organizing, and reading websites is the RSS feed. However, even when you find a feed reader you are comfortable with, the number of resources you receive feeds on can easily get out of hand. For horror resources, then, I suggest you simply use *RA for All: Horror* (mentioned earlier). Figure 14.3 is a screen shot of the main page of *RA for All: Horror.* Note the links on the right that lead to the lists of pages where I continuously compile and organize horror awards, lists, reviews, and resources. Every resource mentioned in this chapter and dozens more are listed with links and brief descriptions so that you can easily look at the wide array of

---

Figure 14.2
Example of a horror author entry written by Becky Spratford for NoveList

Figure 14.3   RA for All: Horror *main page*

RA FOR ALL: HORROR

THE ONLINE HOME OF THE HORROR READERS' ADVISORY, AN ALA PUBLICATION.

WEDNESDAY, JANUARY 12, 2011

Backlist Author Not to Miss: Tananarive Due

One of the great things about working at the public library is that unlike the bookstore, we have many older titles available for checkout.

Horror readers especially, do not care if a book is brand new. They just want something compelling, that makes them feel uneasy, and that will invoke terror. They are among the most willing readers of backlist titles. In my experience as long as the scares are good, they will read anything.

To that end, I am going to start a semi-regular feature here where I will highlight either backlist authors or specific backlist titles. All of these posts will use the label "backlist not to miss," so that you can access all of the posts at one time.

Today I want to highlight the work of Tananarive Due. Due is an author of character driven, suspenseful horror titles that appeal to a wide audience. The tension is palpable and there is violence in her novels, but as horror goes, it is on the less graphic end of the spectrum. The fear and terror are invoked through the oppressive

PAGES

Home

About This Blog

Horror Reviews Index

Horror Publishers

Horror Awards

Horror Resources

Becky's Original Horror Lists

Whole Collection Reading Options

---

web-based horror information with just a few clicks of the mouse. Think of this resource as your portal to the world of horror fiction.

MARKETING YOUR HORROR COLLECTION

Marketing is not just for business school graduates anymore. Librarians have begun to use business and marketing techniques with more savvy. In fact, when I teach readers' advisory in library school, I devote an entire class to marketing issues, including assigning the students a non-library marketing text.[4] With the proliferation of brick-and-mortar bookstores and the popularity of Amazon.com, public libraries have to work even harder now to remind people that they can have all the books they want for *free* at their local library. Marketing campaigns must be forged on two fronts, however. Librarians must first grab the community's interest and bring people into the library, and then they can highlight their collections once patrons are through the door or have accessed the library's website. Horror, specifically, may need a more aggressive marketing campaign than other genres, especially during the eleven months of the year when patrons are not thinking about Halloween. Because it is the rare library that pulls horror out of the main fiction collection, the readers' advisor must find methods for singling horror out from the larger section in which it is embedded. Effective horror marketing will also give you credibility with die-hard horror readers. Once these patrons feel you have a grasp of the genre they love, they tend to open up, asking for assistance with locating materials and even sharing their vast knowledge.

Unfortunately, most libraries only market their horror collections during the month of October. Since you already have a Halloween-primed audience, October is the easiest time of year to highlight your horror offerings. However, you cannot fully capitalize on this interest without highlighting horror at other times of the year as well. Here's a great example of why a one-month, once-a-year display is not enough. Most people in my area visit the library once every three weeks.[5] This visitation rate means your patrons will see your Halloween display once, maybe twice. But where is that display when they come back to return the horror books they just enjoyed? It is already packed up. The horror books are back lurking in the vast general fiction collection, and your readers look elsewhere for their next good read. Marketing in readers' advisory is all about letting patrons know what they would love to read, if only they knew how to find it. Therefore, this section will lay out some ideas and methods to help you make your horror collection shine during any season.

Autumn: File and Save

Throughout September and October, the horror community functions in overdrive. All the horror resources are rushing to put out new information, while there is a flurry of publishing activity in the fall as publishers try to capitalize on Halloween by saturating the market with new horror titles and classic reissues. It is important that you keep a file of everything you find during this prolific and creative time. Websites and ideas you find just days before Halloween may be too late for your holiday-themed marketing but can be used at other times of the year or even next year. I do the most research into horror trends and issues from the end of August into the first two weeks of November. This frenzy makes Halloween both a blessing and a curse. However, if you work hard each autumn, you will not only have a more useful and effective horror collection but also have an easier time marketing that collection all year long.

Horror Lists and Displays: Physical and Virtual

Making lists and putting up displays is the easiest way to market your collection. Patrons love displays because they are easy to browse; however, precisely because they garner a lot of attention, displays need to be thoughtful, well organized, and useful. But when should you put up your horror displays? Obviously, the weeks surrounding Halloween are a great time. I suggest displaying your horror books from October 1 through November 15. This allows people to come in more than once to choose from the display. I also am a big proponent of providing an annotated list highlighting some of the titles patrons can find in your display. This list serves a couple of purposes. One, pulling out a smaller subset of the display gives patrons a taste of what they can find throughout your display. It also shows patrons that you care about helping them find their next good read. Even if they have not stopped at the service desk, you have implicitly shown them that you can be of assistance to them. Two, asking your staff to boil down the appeal of a book in just a few sentences is a great training opportunity. Writing the annotations themselves is a training exercise that results in a product that you can immediately use to help patrons.

In terms of the annotated list for this display, we usually offer two lists of ten books each at the Berwyn Public Library. Each year I create a list highlighting some of our best new horror titles. You can see the 2010 list in figure 14.4.[6] This list is formatted in our display template, and when copied back-to-back, it can be cut down the middle as a bookmark. If you look closely at the list, you'll see I go a step farther than simply annotating the titles—I also offer read-alike suggestions for each title. Readers love options. A list is fine, an annotated list is better, and an annotated list with read-alikes is the best. We also make a list featuring older titles around a certain appeal or subgenre each year to go with the display; in reality, every Halloween patrons are getting twenty suggestions and a display of about one hundred books, right in front of them, without having to sift through the entire collection. I realize, however, that this amount of work may be too much for many libraries without a dedicated RA staff. It is also effective simply to pull out your horror titles and find a way to highlight a few of the newest titles during the Halloween season.

If you do feel adventurous and end up making lists to accompany your displays, remember to also upload them to your website. This is a great marketing tool that requires only a few clicks of the mouse to accomplish. We upload every annotated list we create to our website and file

Figure 14.4   *Example of Becky's Annual Horror Annotations Bookmark with Read-A-Likes*

Horror 2010: Year in Review. It's that time of year again. Scare yourself . . . if you dare!

Campbell, Ramsey. *Creatures of the Pool*
British horror master Campbell's newest novel follows Gavin in his search for his missing father. While delving into his father's research, Gavin uncovers some terrifying secrets about his home-town, secrets that go back centuries. Secrets, suspense, and the supernatural collide in this creepy tale. Also try: *Neverwhere* by Neil Gaiman

Cronin, Justin. *The Passage*
A virus, which turns people into vampires, has decimated North America. Fed up with living in fear, a band of survivors hook up with a mysteriously ageless young girl and attempt to regain control of the world. *The Passage* is an absorbing, frightening, action-packed story which ends with the mother-of-all cliff hangers and a promise of a sequel next year. Also try: *The Stand* by Stephen King

Hill, Joe. *Horns*
In this novel of revenge and demonic possession, Hill adds a unique twist: our hero is turning into the devil. Ig wakes up with horns growing out of his head and has powers to see everyone's deepest and darkest thoughts. Scared of what he is becoming, Ig uses his new dark powers to get revenge for his girlfriend's murder. *Horns* is a thrilling, but unsettling read, as Hill has you rooting for the Devil. Also try: *The One Safe Place* by Ramsey Campbell

Keene, Brian. *Darkness on the Edge of Town*
A small town in Virginia is enveloped in darkness, a darkness from which they cannot escape, a darkness which will kill them if they try to leave. But stuck on the inside, they also become victims to the evil lurking within their town. This is a classic small town horror story with great characters and intensely building suspense. Also try: *Ghost Road Blues* by Jonathan Maberry

Kenyon, Nate. *Sparrow Rock*
Six teenagers survive a nuclear bomb explosion in an underground bunker. As they await rescue, things go from bad to worse. First, they may not have been in the bomb shelter by accident and then, mutant bugs begin turning everyone into zombies. Should they stay locked underground, or attempt to make it on the outside. This is a heart-pounding, edge-of-your-seat read. Also try: *The Ruins* by Scott Smith

Lamberson, Gregory. *The Frenzy Way*
A murderer is on the loose in NYC, but it is no man Police Captain Mace is chasing, it is a werewolf. With the help of three supernatural investigators, Mace and his motley crew track the werewolf and try to stop him before too many people die. This is a fast-paced, terrifyingly bloody, and ultimately satisfying tale. Also try: *Sharp Teeth* by Toby Barlow

McCrary, Michelle and Joe McKinney, eds.
Dead Set: A Zombie Anthology
With 2010 being proclaimed as the Year of the Zombie, what better way to celebrate than with this collection of zombie tales by some of the genre's best writers including Ben Vincent and Harry Shannon. Also try: *Feed* by Mira Grant

Ochse, Weston. *Empire of Salt*
Speaking of zombies . . . Bombay Beach, California is not a prosperous town; it smells, there are lots of earthquakes, and it is populated by the dregs of civilizations, and that is without considering the hordes of zombies running rampant. Ochse plays off of the common horror setting of the isolated town and then lets the zombies loose. Good, gory, zombie fun. Also try: *The Rising* by Brian Keene

Strand, Jeff. *Dweller*
Toby is an outcast who finds peace in the deep woods behind his home. He also finds a monster living there—a monster named Owen, who becomes Toby's best friend for over 50 years. But when your best friend is an actual monster, he can inflict horrible things on your enemies. This is an original, heart-breaking and chilling story. Also try: *My Soul to Keep* by Tananarive Due

Straub, Peter. *A Dark Matter*
In 1966 four friends participate in an occult ceremony that had gruesome circumstances. As adults, they come together to recount their experiences, realizing that their childhood game might have unleashed an evil force onto the world. Also try: *The Burning* by Bentley Little

them under the heading Suggested Reading Lists.[7] Patrons love this link. They come in and say something like, "Remember when you had that list on . . . ?" and we can show them how they can literally go back in time and get the list again. At the RA desk we believe in the product we are creating and want to allow patrons access to it at any time. These lists take mere seconds to upload and use up very little server space. Considering the huge marketing and customer service boost our Suggested Reading Lists give us, this tool is a no-brainer. I have also found that staff members work harder on their annotated display lists knowing that those lists will live on in perpetuity on the website.

Post-Halloween Horror

What about the rest of the year? There are a few ways to market your horror offerings beyond Halloween. The first and most obvious suggestion is to have a horror display at another time of year. There is no law that horror books can only be in the spotlight in the fall. Why not use the summer release of a new horror movie or TV show as an excuse to showcase your horror book holdings? Another popular idea is to pull popular horror films and the books on which they were based for a cross-format display. We also like to build displays around popular authors. For example, when Stephen King has a new book and the waiting list is in the hundreds, you can pull read-alike options and simply place the books anywhere you can find the space. A quick sign reminding people to place their holds on the newest King and offering them a similar title while they wait should do the trick. This kind of "read-alike" display is a great way to showcase the full breadth of your horror offerings. The point of these examples is to think outside the Halloween box. You can make horror displays during other times of the year, and people will read the books. Too many people check out horror books every October for you to deny that people like horror. Why not remind your patrons of your horror offerings more than once a year?

Working Horror In Every Day

Even more effective than a second horror display is working horror into your more general marketing. In the Readers' Advisory Department at the Berwyn Public Library, we make a conscious effort to represent as many genres as possible in all our displays and lists. For example, if the theme is Back to School, we have titles with academic settings in many categories, including literary fiction, thriller, mystery, romance, horror, and more, all on display together. In our annotated list accompanying the display, we highlight a range of genres. This practice serves two purposes. One, it attracts the widest audience possible to our display. And two, it reminds patrons of the range of books we have to offer.

You can market horror in more than just displays. We have an ongoing staff recommendation shelf called the Browser's Corner. It is both a physical corner in the library and a virtual one online (http://browserscorner. wordpress.com). The actual shelf has a rotating collection of books, placed face out, with shelf talkers hanging below. These shelf talkers are written by library staff and focus on the appeal of the book. Online in the *Browser's Corner* blog, the descriptions are regularly uploaded. And because the blog is not limited by physical shelf space, all descriptions are available at all times. They are also searchable by appeal. One reason the Browser's Corner is so popular is that staff members go out of their way to include a wide range of titles. You can find every genre represented, including horror. The point is, by including horror as a regular part of our ongoing staff recommendations, we are implicitly telling our patrons that it is just as important as any other genre, all year long.

Read-Alikes

Another service that we offer all readers, including horror fans, is a data bank of author read-alikes. These titles are housed on our web page and listed alphabetically by author. We do not separate them by genre, so readers can browse all of them at once. Figure 14.5 is a screen shot of the entry for Stephen King. All links go to the catalog record for that author. We use these read-alike lists to create the "While you wait . . ." displays mentioned earlier and to help us prepare for big-name releases. When a patron comes in for the newest Stephen King and realizes there is a wait, our staff members are ready to offer another book immediately. We try to have read-alike lists for the most popular authors at our library available online for patrons to use themselves. This online availability shows readers that we are anticipating their needs. And again, horror authors are included with all other genres. They are there all year long, interfiled with everyone else, just waiting for the right reader to find them.

The message I have been arguing throughout this entire marketing discussion is that no matter what you do to highlight any part of your collection, the effort must be forged on two fronts, both physically, in the library building, and virtually, on your website. In fact, no issue is more

Figure 14.5   *Example of Read-Alike Authors page from the Berwyn (Illinois) Public Library website*

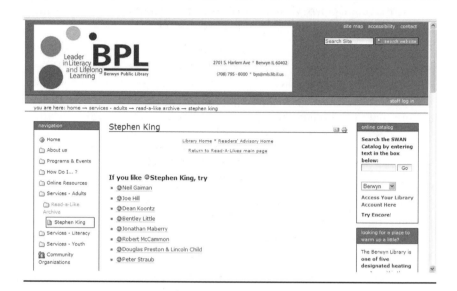

important to public libraries today than providing both physical and virtual access to the library.

FINAL THOUGHTS

All the tips, resources, and advice in this chapter are here to remind you how you can best assist your horror patrons. I have found over the years, however, that some librarians are scared of helping horror readers, mostly because of how scary the books themselves are. To these librarians I say, you do not need to like horror books to help horror readers. You simply need to understand the genre and be able to use the tools. I have armed you well for battle throughout this book, and you no longer have anything to fear. At this point, you may even know enough to stop an actual pack of zombies. The easiest thing is to simply remember that your horror patrons are not monsters, they just like to read about them.

NOTES

1. Ellen Datlow's Best Horror of the Year series comes out each March. The 2010 edition was *The Best Horror of the Year, Volume 2* (San Francisco: Night Shade Books, 2010).

2. This now defunct series ended in 2008 with *The Year's Best Fantasy and Horror 2008: 21st Annual Collection*, ed. Ellen Datlow (New York: St. Martin's Griffin, 2008).

3. NoveList is a fee-based database owned by EBSCO. I get access with my Berwyn Public Library card. Go to www.ebsco.com for more information.

4. In GSLIS 763 at Dominican University, I assign sections from Paco Underhill, *Why We Buy: The Science of Shopping* (New York: Simon and Schuster, 2009).

5. Paco Underhill's company, Envirosell, conducted a study of libraries in the Metropolitan Library System (Illinois). The project was titled "The Customer Focused Library." The results and final report, including the statistics about the frequency of library visits, can be viewed at www.mls.lib.il.us/consulting/envirosell.asp. A print copy is available by request to Becky Spratford.

6. For previous years' lists go to Becky's Original Horror Lists on *RA for All: Horror,* http://raforallhorror.blogspot.com/p/beckys-original-horror-lists.html.

7. The Suggested Reading Lists can be found at www.berwynlibrary.org/adult-services/suggested-reading-lists.html.

BIBLIOGRAPHY

A.K.A.: Author Pseudonyms, Aliases, Nicknames, Working Names, Legalized Names, Pen Names, Noms de Plume, Maiden Names . . . Etc. http://trussel.com/books/pseudo.htm.

Amazon.com. http://amazon.com.

Ashley, Mike. *Who's Who in Horror and Fantasy Fiction.* New York: Taplinger, 1977.

AudioFile: The Magazine for People Who Love Audiobooks. http:// audiofilemagazine.com.

Barclay, Glen St. John. *Anatomy of Horror: The Masters of Occult Fiction.* New York: St. Martin's Press, 1978.

Barron, Neil, ed. *Fantasy and Horror: A Critical and Historical Guide to Literature, Illustration, Film, TV, Radio, and the Internet.* Lanham, MD: Scarecrow, 1999.

———. *Horror Literature: A Reader's Guide.* New York: Garland, 1990.

Bloom, Harold, ed. *Modern Critical Views: Stephen King.* Philadelphia: Chelsea House, 1998.

Booklist Online: Book Reviews from the American Library Association. www.booklistonline.com.

Castle, Mort, ed. *On Writing Horror, Revised Edition: A Handbook by the Horror Writers Association.* Cincinnati, OH: Writer's Digest Books, 2007.

Clark, Donia. "From Dracula to Hannibal: Escaping into Horror." *ILA Reporter* 10, no. 4 (August 2002): 10–11.

Collings, Michael R. *Scaring Us to Death: The Impact of Stephen King on Popular Culture.* The Milford Series: Popular Writers of Today 63. San Bernardino, CA: Borgo, 1997.

Dark Scribe Magazine. www.darkscribemagazine.com.

Datlow, Ellen, ed. *The Best Horror of the Year, Volume 1.* Portland, OR: Night Shade Books, 2009.

————. *The Best Horror of the Year, Volume 2.* San Francisco: Night Shade Books, 2010.

Douglas, Drake. *Horrors!* New York: Overlook Press, 1989.

Everson, William K. *Classics of the Horror Film.* New York: Citadel, 1990.

Fantastic Fiction. www.fantasticfiction.co.uk.

Fiction_L (electronic discussion list). www.webrary.org/rs/flmenu.html.

Fonseca, Anthony J., and June Michelle Pulliam. *Hooked on Horror III: A Guide to Reading Interests in Horror Fiction.* Westport, CT: Libraries Unlimited, 2009.

Frank, Alan G. *The Movie Treasury: Horror Movies; Tales of Terror in the Cinema.* London: Octopus Books, 1974.

Frank, Frederick S. *Through the Pale Door: A Guide to and through the American Gothic.* New York: Greenwood, 1990.

Golden, Christopher. *Cut! Horror Writers on Horror Films.* New York: Berkley, 1992.

Greenberg, Martin, Ed Gorman, and Bill Munster. *The Dean Koontz Companion.* New York: Berkley, 1994.

Greenfieldt, John. *Fiction Core Collection.* New York: H. W. Wilson, 2010.

Herald, Diana Tixier. *Genreflecting: A Guide to Popular Reading Interests.* Westport, CT: Libraries Unlimited, 2006.

Hester, Patrick. "Whatever Happened to Scary Vampires." *SF Signal.* www.sfsignal.com/archives/2010/09/draft-i-miss-scary-vampires/. Originally posted September 27, 2010.

Horror Blogger Alliance. http://horrorbloggeralliance.blogspot.com.

Horror Fiction Review. http://thehorrorfictionreview.blogspot.com/.

Horror World. www.horrorworld.org.

Horror Writers Association. www.horror.org.

International Thriller Writers. http://thrillerwriters.org.

Jones, Stephen, and Kim Newman, eds. *Horror: The Best 100 Books.* New York: Carroll and Graf, 1998.

King, Stephen. *Danse Macabre.* New York: Everest House, 1981.

————. *On Writing: A Memoir of the Craft.* New York: Scribner, 2000.

Knost, Michael, ed. *Writers Workshop of Horror.* Breinigsville, PA: Woodland Press, 2009.

Kotker, Joan G. *Dean Koontz: A Critical Companion.* Westport, CT: Greenwood Press, 1996.

Library Journal. www.libraryjournal.com.

Literature Resource Center (subscription service). http://infotrac .galegroup.com. Gale Cengage Learning.

Monster Librarian. www.monsterlibrarian.com.

NoveList (subscription service). http://search.epnet.com. EBSCO Publishing.

Ottinger, John, III. "Brains Lite: A Brief and Incomplete History of Zombie Literature." *Electric Velocipede,* Issue 21/22 (Fall 2010).

———. "An Interview with Jonathan Maberry." Strange Horizons. www.strangehorizons.com/2010/20100816/maberry-a.shtml. Originally posted August 16, 2010.

Pawuk, Michael. *Graphic Novels: A Genre Guide to Comic Books, Manga, and More.* Westport, CT: Libraries Unlimited, 2007.

Perry, Janet, and Victor Gentle. *Zombies.* Milwaukee, WI: Gareth Stevens, 1999.

Poe, Edgar Allan. *The Complete Tales and Poems of Edgar Allan Poe.* New York: Castle Books, 2002.

Pringle, David, ed. *St. James Guide to Horror, Ghost and Gothic Writers.* Detroit: St. James Press, 1998.

Publishers Weekly. www.publishersweekly.com/pw/home/index.html.

Pulliam, June Michelle, and Anthony Fonseca. *Read On . . . Horror Fiction.* Westport, CT: Libraries Unlimited, 2006.

Punter, David. *The Literature of Terror: A History of Gothic Fiction from 1765 to the Present Day.* New York: Longman, 1996.

RA for All. http://raforall.blogspot.com.

RA for All: Horror. http://raforallhorror.blogspot.com.

Saricks, Joyce. *The Readers' Advisory Guide to Genre Fiction.* Chicago: ALA Editions, 2009.

———. *Readers' Advisory Service in the Public Library.* 3rd ed. Chicago: ALA Editions, 2005.

Skal, David J. *The Monster Show: A Cultural History of Horror.* New York: W. W. Norton, 1993.

Stacey, Jan, and Ryder Syvertsen. *The Great Book of Movie Monsters.* Chicago: Contemporary Books, 1993.

Stuprich, Michael, ed. *The Greenhaven Press Companion to Literary Movements and Genres: Horror.* San Diego: Greenhaven Press, 2001.

System Wide Automated Network (SWAN). Burr Ridge, IL: Metropolitan Library System Catalog. http://swan.mls.lib.il.us/search.

Twitchell, James B. *Dreadful Pleasures: An Anatomy of Modern Horror.* New York: Oxford University Press, 1985.

Tymn, Marshall B. *Horror Literature: A Core Collection and Reference Guide.* New York: R. R. Bowker, 1981.

Warner, Matthew. *Horror Isn't a 4-Letter Word: Essays on Writing and Appreciating the Genre.* Hyattsville, MD: Guide Dog Books, 2008.

Weiner, Stephen. *The 101 Best Graphic Novels.* New York: NBM, 2005.

Weird Tales: The Original Magazine of the Unique, Fantastic, and the Bizarre. http://weirdtalesmagazine.com.

Winter, Douglas E., ed. *Prime Evil: New Stories by the Masters of Modern Horror.* New York: American Library, 1998.

INDEX

A

Abraham Lincoln: Vampire Hunter (Grahame-Smith), 67–68
Abrahams, Peter, 33, 129
academic frame, 25
Acevedo, Mario, 120
Adams, John Joseph, 76
adjectives, use of, 20
Agarwal, Shilpa, 59
Alliance (blog), 142
Amazon.com (marketing), 144
Amazonia (Rollins), 131
American Vampire series (Snyder and King), 133
Ancestor (Sigler), 98
ancient evil. *See* monsters and ancient evil
Anderson, Kevin David, 120
Anderson, Kevin J., 120–121
Apocalypse of the Dead (McKinney), 80
appeal, horror and
application of, 23–26
characters, 19–20
frame and setting, 22–23
language and style, 20–21
pacing, 20
story line, 21–22
tone and mood, 18–19
Armstrong, Kelley, 17
audiobooks, 134
Austen, Jane
Northanger Abbey, 3
Pride and Prejudice, ix
authors
established, 35–40
new generation, 32–35
pulp horror, 40–43
women writers, 43–45
Await Your Reply (Chaon), 129

B

The Bad Seed (March), 53
Bag of Bones (King), 61
Baldacci, David, 17
Barker, Clive
Halloween, 8
The Hellbound Heart, 112, 114
Hellraiser, 8
key horror author, 9
Nightmare on Elm Street, movie series, 8
Satan and demonic possession, 112
Barlow, Toby, 85
Basilisk (Masterton), 96–97
Bear, Greg, 59
The Beast House (Laymon), 96
Becker, Robin M., 121
Bell, Alden, 77, 129
Benchley, Peter, 7
Benjamin's Parasite (Strand), 124
Berserk (Lebbon), 79
The Best Horror of the Year (Datlow), 135
Best Horror of the Year series (Datlow), 140
Bierce, Ambrose, 5
Birch, A. G., 7
Bite Marks: A Vampire Testament (Taylor), 72
The Black Carousel (Grant), 95
Black Creek Crossing (Saul), 107
Black House (King and Straub), 46
Black Magic Woman (Gustainis), 104–105
Blackwood, Algernon, 5
Blackwood Farm (Rice), 71
The Blair Witch Project (film), 136
Blatty, William Peter, 7, 50, 112
Bleiler, E. F., 7
Bloch, Robert, 7
blogs, marketing and, 149

Blood and Gold (Rice), 71
Blood and Ice (Masello), 131
Blood Canticle (Rice), 71
Blood Lite (Anderson), 120–121
Bloodstone (Kenyon), 105
The Book of Fate (Meltzer), 29
bookmarks, marketing and, 147
Bradbury, Ray
    horror author, 7
    pulp-era author, 6
    Something Wicked This Way Comes,
        50–51
Brains: A Zombie Memoir (Becker), 121
Bram Stoker Award, 8
Braunbeck, Gary
    Coffin County, 42
    Far Dark Fields, 93
    Keepers, 85
    major horror author of 21st century,
        10
    pulp horror and, 41–42
Breathers: A Zombie's Lament (Browne),
        27, 121
Breeding Ground (Pinborough), 88
Brimstone (Preston and Child), 134
Brides of the Impaler (Lee), 68–69
Brontë, Charlotte, 3
Brontë, Emily, 3, 51, 57
Brooks, Max, 10
    World War Z, 77, 134
    The Zombie Survival Guide, 132
Browne, S. G., 27, 121
Buchan, John, 103
Buffy the Vampire Slayer (television
        series), 136
Bull, Emma, 130
Burrow, B. J., 121
Butcher, Jim, 9, 17, 39, 130

C
Campbell, Ramsey
    authors similar to, 37
    Creatures of the Pool, 93–94
    The Darkest Part of the Woods,
        103–104
    The Grin of the Dark, 94
    major horror author, 9

Nazareth Hill, 59–60
Pact of the Fathers, 104
The Caretaker of Lorne Field (Zeltserman),
        89
Carmilla (Le Fanu), 52
Carrie (King), 1, 7, 49
Carroll, Jonathan, 130
Castaways (Keene), 23–26
Casting the Runes and Other Ghost Stories
        (James), 52
The Castle of Los Angeles (Morton), 44
The Castle of Otranto (Walpole), 2, 54, 57
Catching Hell (Gifune), 114
Cave, Hugh, 7
Cell (King), 78
Chambers, Robert W., 5
Chaney, Lon Jr., 6
The Changed (Burrow), 121
Chaon, Dan, 129
characters, horror and, 19–20
Child, Lincoln
    Brimstone, 134
    Pendergast novels, 131
A Choir of Ill Children (Piccirilli), 107
Christine (King), 112
The City and the City (Miéville), 130
City of the Dead (Keene), 115
Clark, Simon
    The Day of the Triffids, 85
    Ghost Monster, 114
    The Night of the Triffids, 85
    This Rage of Echoes, 94
    Vampyrrhic, 67
classic horror
    characteristics of, 49–50
    titles, 50–55
Classic Radio Horror, 134
classic titles, 49–55
Clegg, Douglas, 9
    Mischief, 60
    Naomi, 103
    You Come When I Call You, 94
Coffin County (Braunbeck), 42
collections, 127–136
    marketing of, 144–150
Collins, Wilkie, 3
Come Closer (Gran), 115

comic horror, 26–27
  characteristics of, 119–120
  titles, 120–125
coming-of-age theme, 21
Conjure Wife (Leiber), 106
Conlon, Christopher, 135
The Conqueror Worms (Keene), 87
Cooper, Seamus, 121
Corsaro, Frank, 114
Covenant (Everson), 41
Craven, Wes, 119
Creatures of the Pool (Campbell), 93–94
Cree Black series (Hecht), 131
Creepers (Morrell), 131
Crichton, Michael, 131
Crimson (Rollo), 117
Cronin, Justin, 16, 67
The Cryptopedia (Maberry and Kramer), 132
Cthulhu Mythos stories, 5
Cujo (King), 87
Cycle of the Werewolf (King), 87

D
Dahl, Roald, 7
Danielewski, Mark Z., 114
Danse Macabre (King), 132
Dark Delicacies series (Howison and Gelb), 135
dark fantasy
  characteristics, 129
  titles, 130
Dark Hollow (Keene), 61
Dark Harvest (Partridge), 97
A Dark Matter (Straub), 108
Dark Mountain (Laymon), 105
Dark Places (Flynn), 129
Dark Scribe Magazine, 42, 140–141
Dark Sister (Joyce), 105
Dark Tower series (King), 8
Darker Angels (Somtow), 80–81
The Darkest Part of the Woods (Campbell), 103–104
Darkly Dreaming Dexter (Lindsay), 129
Datlow, Ellen
  Best Horror of the Year series, 140
  The Best Horror of the Year, 135

Haunted Legends, 60
Inferno, 135
The Day of the Triffids (Clark), 85
de la Mare, Walter, 5
de Lint, Charles, 9
Dead City (McKinney), 80
Dead Lines (Bear), 59
Death: A Life (Pendle), 123–124
Deathbringer (Smith), 80
Death's Excellent Vacation, 123
Deaver, Jeffery, 39
Deeper (Long), 117
del Toro, Guillermo, 131
Delaney, Matthew, 94
Demon-Hunting Soccer Mom series (Kenner), 17
demonic possession. *See* Satan and demonic possession
Depraved (Smith), 98
Derleth, August, 7
Descendant (Masterton), 69
The Descent (Long), 116–117
Desperate Souls (Lamberson), 78–79
Dexter (television series), 136
Dickens, Charles, 3
Different Kinds of Darkness (Langford), 123
A Dirty Job (Moore), 123
displays, marketing and, 146
Dobyns, Stephen, 37
Donohue, Keith, 134
Doyle, Arthur Conan, 51
Dracula (film), 136
Dracula (Stoker), 1, 4, 54, 65–66
Dracula: The Un-Dead (Stoker and Holt), 71
Dresden Files, series (Butcher), ix, 17, 130
Drood (Simmons), 134
du Maurier, Daphne, 7, 51
Due, Tananarive
  The Good House, 95
  major horror author, 9
  My Soul to Keep, 94–95
Dunbar, Robert
  Martyrs and Monsters, 46
  The Pines, 42, 95
  The Shore, 95

The Dunwich Horror and Others (Lovecraft), 53
Dust (Turner), 81
Dweller (Strand), 46, 98
Dziemianowicz, Stephen, 104

E

Edgar Allan Poe Audio Collection (Poe), 134
Egolf, Tristan, 122
emotion, manipulation of, 13–14
Empire of Salt (Ochse), 80
End of Story (Abrahams), 129
Enlightenment, examples
    Dracula, 4
    Frankenstein, 4
    The Island of Dr. Moreau, 4
    key authors, 5
    The Strange Case of Dr. Jekyll and Mr. Hyde, 4
Entertainment Weekly (magazine), 36
Everson, John
    Covenant, 41
    major horror author, 10
    Sacrifice, 104
evil, ancient. *See* monsters and ancient evil
The Exorcist (Blatty)
    classic horror, 50
    pulp-era movie, 7, 136
    Satan and demonic possession, 112

F

factors, horror appeal, 19
Faerie Tale (Feist), 130
Fangland (Marks), 69
Fang-tastic Fiction (Mathews), 67
fantasy, dark, 129–130
Far Dark Fields (Braunbeck), 93
Farris, John
    High Bloods, 85
    major horror author, 9
    Phantom Nights, 60–61
    You Don't Scare Me, 95
Fat White Vampire Blues (Fox), 122
Feed (Grant), ix, 17
Feist, Raymond, 130

Fiction Core Collection (Jones and Newman), 50
A Field Guide to Demons, Fairies, Fallen Angels, and Other Subversive Spirits (Mack), 132
The 5th Witch (Masterton), 106
films and television series, 136
Finch (VanderMeer), 130
Fingerman, Bob, 77
Fires Rising (Laimo), 116
flashbacks, style and, 20–21
Floating Dragon (Straub), 98
Flynn, Gillian, 129
Fonseca, Anthony J.
    Hooked on Horror III, 50, 140
    Read On . . . Horror Fiction, 140
The Forbidden Zone (Strieber), 89
Fox, Andrew, 122
frame and setting, horror and, 22–23
Frankenstein (Shelley)
    classic horror, 53–54
    end of Gothic era, 3
    Enlightenment influence, 4
The Frenzy Way (Lamberson), 87
Frostbite (Wellington), 89

G

Gagliani, W. D., 85–86
Gaiman, Neil
    The Graveyard Book, 134
    Neverwhere, 130
    Sandman series, 133
    Stories: All-New Tales, 135
Garton, Ray
    Live Girls, 67
    The Loveliest Dead, 60
    Ravenous, 86
Gates, R. Patrick, 102, 104
A Gathering of Crows (Keene), 87
Geillor, Harrison, 122
Gelb, Jeff, 135
genres
    monsters, 16–17
    paranormal, 15–16
    serial killers, 16
    zombies, 17

Ghost Monster (Clark), 114
Ghost Radio (Gout), 60, 134
Ghost Road Blues (Maberry), 34, 96
Ghost Story (Straub), 36–37, 63
ghosts and haunted houses
    characteristics of, 57–59
    key authors, 5
    titles, 59–64
Ghoul (Keene), 95
Gifune, Greg F., 10, 114
Gil's All Fright Diner (Martinez), 123
Golden, Christopher
    major horror author, 9
    The New Dead, 77
    Wildwood Road, 114–115
Goldsher, Alan, 122
Goldsmith, Francisca, 133
The Golem (Lee), 96
Gonzalez, J. F., 86
The Good House (Due), 95
Goshgarian, Gary, 104
Gospel of the Living Dead (Paffenroth), 132
Gothic novels
    The Castle of Otranto, 2
    Jane Eyre, 3
    key authors, 3
    The Monk, 2
    Mysteries of Udolpho, 3
    Northanger Abbey, 3
    The Vampyre, 2
    Wuthering Heights, 3
Gout, Leopoldo, 60, 134
Grahame-Smith, Seth, 67–68, 119–120, 122–123
Gran, Sara, 115
Grant, Charles, 9, 37, 95
Grant, Mira, ix, 17, 131
graphic novels, 133
Graphic Novels (Pawuk), 133
The Graveyard Book (Gaiman), 134
Greenberg, Martin H., 104
Greer, John Michael, 132
Gregory, Daryl, 115
Grimm Memorials (Gates), 102, 104
The Grin of the Dark (Campbell), 94
Gustainis, Justin, 104–105

H
Halloween (film), 8, 136
Halloween, marketing beyond, 148
Handling the Undead (Lindqvist), 79
Harris, Charlaine
    Death's Excellent Vacation, 123
    Gothic-style novels, 3
    Sookie Stackhouse series, 9, 66
The Harrowing (Sokoloff), 44, 63
Harry Dresden series (Butcher), 9, 39
Haunted America (Norman and Scott), 132
haunted houses. *See* ghosts and haunted houses
Haunted Legends (Datlow and Mamatas), 60
Haunting Bombay (Agarwal), 59
The Haunting of Hill House (Jackson), 52
Hawthorne, Nathaniel, 3, 51
He Is Legend (Conlon), 135
Heart-Shaped Box (Hill), 32, 61
Hecht, Daniel, 131
The Hellbound Heart (Barker), 112, 114
Hellboy series (Mignola), 133
Hellraiser (modern horror movie), 8
Her Fearful Symmetry (Niffenegger), 130
High Bloods (Farris), 85
Highsmith, Patricia, 129
Hill, Joe
    Heart-Shaped Box, 61
    Horns, 46, 112, 115
    Locke and Key series, 133
    major horror author, 10
    new-generation horror, 32–33
The Historian (Kostova), 68
history of horror
    about, 1–2
    beginning of modern horror, 7–9
    the Enlightenment, 3–5
    future of, 10
    ghost stories, 5–6
    Gothic novels, 2–3
    new millennium of, 9–10
    pulp era, 6–7
The Hitchhiker (television series), 136
Hoffman, E. T. A., 3
Hogan, Chuck, 131

Holland, David, 86
Hollands, Neil, 15
Holt, Ian, 71
Hooked on Horror III (Fonseca and Pulliam), 50, 140
Horns (Hill), 32, 112, 115
horror
  as an emotion, 13–14
  appeal of, 13–28
  classics of, 49–55
  collection options, 127–136
  comic horror, 119–125
  defined, 13, 14
  ghosts and haunted houses, 57–63
  history of, 1–10
  monsters and ancient evil, 91–100
  need for, ix–x
  reference guide for, 31–45
  resources and marketing, 139–150
  Satan and demonic possession, 111–118
  shape-shifters and, 83–90
  trends in, 26–27
  twentieth-century authors, 7
  vampires and, 16–17, 65–73
  witches and the occult, 101–109
  zombies and, 75–81
Horror: The 100 Best Books (Jones and Newman), 50
horror authors
  Enlightenment, 5
  ghost story, 5
  Gothic, 3
  modern, 9
  twentieth century, 7
  twenty-first century, 10
The Horror Fiction Review (blog), 141
horror films, 136
Horror in the Air (Classic Radio Horror), 134
Horror Isn't a 4-Letter Word (Warner), 140
horror novels, identifying
  appeal of, 18–23
  applying appeal, 23–26
  defining horror, 13–15

horror *vs.* non-horror, 17
  paranormal fiction, 15–16
  serial killers, 16
  traditional monsters, 16–17
horror television series, 136
Horror World (web community), 141
Horror Writers Association, 8, 141
A House Divided (LeBlanc), 44, 62
House of Blood (Smith), 63
House of Bones (Masterton), 62
House of Leaves (Danielewski), 114
The House of the Seven Gables (Hawthorne), 51
Howison, Del, 135
Hubbard, L. Ron, 7
The Hunger (Strieber), 72
Huston, Charlie, 131
Huxley, T. H., 3

I

In the Night Room (Straub), 63
Infected (Sigler), 134
Inferno (Datlow), 135
Interview with a Vampire (Rice), 8, 16, 66, 70
The Invisible Man (Wells), 54–55
Irving, Washington, 51–52
The Island of Dr. Moreau (Wells), 4
isolated frame, 25

J

Jackson, Shirley
  The Haunting of Hill House, 52
  horror author, 7
  pulp-era author, 6
Jacobs, W. W., 5
James, Henry
  Gothic novels and, 3, 5
  The Turn of the Screw, 52, 57, 129
James, M. R., 5, 52
Jane Eyre (Brontë), 3
Jaws (film), 136
Jinn (Delaney), 94
Joe Pitt series (Huston), 131
John Dies at the End (Wong), 124
Jones, Stephen, 50
Joyce, Graham, 105

K

Karloff, Boris, 6

Keene, Brian
    Castaways, 23–26, 41, 95
    as character-centered author, 35
    City of the Dead, 115
    The Conqueror Worms, 87
    Dark Hollow, 61
    A Gathering of Crows, 87
    Ghoul, 95
    major horror author, 10
    The Rising, 41, 77–78

The Keep (Wilson), 71, 72

The Keeper (Langan), 61

Keepers (Braunbeck), 85

Kelner, Toni L. P., 123

Kenner, Julie, 17

Kent, Jasper, 68

Kenyon, Nate
    Bloodstone, 105
    major horror author, 10
    pulp horror and, 41
    The Reach, 116
    Sparrow Rock, 17, 47, 78

Kenyon, Sherrilyn, ix

Ketchum, Jack, 9, 95

Kiernan, Caitlin
    The Red Tree, 45, 87
    women horror authors, 45

King, Stephen
    American Vampire series, 133
    authors similar to, 36
    Bag of Bones, 61
    Black House, 46
    Carrie, 1, 7, 49
    Cell, 78
    Christine, 112
    Cujo, 87
    Cycle of the Werewolf, 87
    Danse Macabre, 132
    Dark Tower series, 8
    as established author, 35–36
    ghost story author, 5
    Joe Hill and, 10, 32–33
    key horror author, 9
    The Mist, 134
    Pet Sematary, 78

'Salem's Lot, 68

The Shining, 36, 61

The Stand, 36, 47

The Talisman, 47

The Tommyknockers, 61

Kirkman, Robert, 78, 133

Knipfel, Jim, 130

Koontz, Dean
    established horror author, 38–39
    Horror Writers of America and, 8
    key horror author, 9
    Watchers, 38, 47

Kornwolf (Egolf), 122

Kostova, Elizabeth, 68

Kramer, David F., 132

Kunma (Corsaro), 114

L

Laimo, Michael
    Fires Rising, 116
    major horror author, 10
    Satan and demonic possession, 112

Lamberson, Gregory
    Desperate Souls, 78–79
    The Frenzy Way, 87

The Land of Laughs (Carroll), 130

Langan, John, 135

Langan, Sarah
    The Keeper, 61
    major horror author, 10
    The Missing, 79
    women horror authors, 43–44

Langford, David, 123

language and style, horror and, 20–21

Lansdale, Joe
    Horror Writers of America and, 8
    key horror author, 9
    Retro Pulp Tales series, 135

Lasher (Rice), 107

The Last Man on Earth (film), 136

Last Things (Searcy), 97–98

The Last Vampire (Strieber), 72

Layman, John, 133

Laymon, Richard
    The Beast House, 96
    Dark Mountain, 105
    major horror author, 9

The Traveling Vampire Show, 68
To Wake the Dead, 96
The Woods Are Dark, 96
Le Fanu, Joseph Sheridan, 3, 52
Lebbon, Tim, 79
LeBlanc, Deborah
  A House Divided, 44, 62
  major horror author of the 21st
    century, 10
  Water Witch, 105
Lee, Edward
  Brides of the Impaler, 68–69
  The Golem, 96
  major horror author, 10
  The Messenger, 116
  Slither, 87–88
The Legend of Sleepy Hollow (Irving),
    51–52
Leiber, Fritz, 7, 106
Let Me In (Lindqvist), 69
Let the Right One In (Lindqvist), 69
Levin, Ira, 7, 53
Lewis, Matthew
  Gothic author, 3
  The Monk, 2
Library Journal, 127
Lilith's Dream (Strieber), 72
Lindqvist, John Ajvide, 69, 79
Lindsay, Jeff, 129
lists, marketing and, 146
Little, Bentley
  major horror author, 9
  The Return, 96
  The Town, 116
  The Walking, 79–80
The Little Stranger (Waters), 129
Live Girls (Garton), 67
The Living Dead (Adams), 76
The Living Dead 2 (Adams), 76
Locke and Key series (Hill), 133
Long, Jeff, 116–117
Lovecraft, H. P.
  Cthulhu Mythos stories, 5
  The Dunwich Horror and Others, 53
  horror author, 7
  pulp era and, 6
  Tales of the Cthulhu Mythos, 135

The Loveliest Dead (Garton), 60
Lugosi, Bela, 6
Lumley, Brian, 9

M
Maberry, Jonathan
  The Cryptopedia, 132
  Ghost Road Blues, 34, 96
  major horror author, 10
  new-generation horror, 34–35
  Rot and Ruin, 80
  The Wolfman, 88
Machen, Arthur, 5
Mack, Carol K., 132
The Magician (Maugham), 106
The Mall of Cthulhu (Cooper), 121
Mamatas, Nick, 60
Manitou Blood (Masterton), 69
March, William, 7, 53
marketing, autumn, 145
Marks, John, 69
Martinez, A. Lee, 123
Martyrs and Monsters (Dunbar), 42
Marvel Zombies vs. Army of Darkness
    series (Layman), 133
Masello, Robert, 10, 131
Masters of Horror (television series),
    136
Masterton, Graham
  Basilisk, 96–97
  Descendant, 69
  The 5th Witch, 106
  House of Bones, 62
  major horror author, 9
  Manitou Blood, 69
Matheson, Richard
  horror author, 7
  pulp-era author, 6
Mathews, Patricia O'Brien, 67
Maugham, W. Somerset, 106
Mayfair Witches series (Rice), 107
McCammon, Robert
  Horror Writers of America and, 8
  key horror author, 9
  The Wolf's Hour, 88
McKinney, Joe
  Apocalypse of the Dead, 80

Dead City, 80
    major horror author, 10
Melton, J. Gordon, 132
Meltzer, Brad, 17, 29
Memnoch the Devil (Rice), 70
Merrick (Rice), 71
The Messenger (Lee), 116
The Midnight Guardian (Stratford), 45
Midnight Mass (Wilson), 72
The Midnight Road (Piccirilli), 131
Midnight Walk (Morton), 135
Miéville, China, 130
Mignola, Mike, 133
Mischief (Clegg), 60
The Missing (Langan), 43, 79
The Mist (King), 134
Mitchell, Mary Ann, 106
The Monk (Lewis), 2
Monster (Peretti), 97
Monster Librarian (website), 141
monster revolt *vs.* horror, 16–17
Monster trilogy (Wellington), 81
monsters and ancient evil
    characteristics of, 91–93
    titles, 93–100
mood and tone, 18–19
Moore, Alan, 133
Moore, Christopher
    comic horror, 119
    A Dirty Job, 123
    major horror author, 9
    You Suck, 119
Morrell, David, 35, 131
Morton, Lisa, 44, 135
Mostert, Natasha, 106
Mr. Gaunt and Other Uneasy Encounters
    (Langan), 135
The Mummy (pulp-era movie), 6
Murcheston: The Wolf's Tale (Holland), 86
My Soul to Keep (Due), 94–95
Mysteries of Udolpho (Radcliffe), 3

N

Naomi (Clegg), 103
Nathaniel (Saul), 62
Nazareth Hill (Campbell), 37, 59–60
Neverwhere (Gaiman), 130

The New Dead (Golden), 77
The New Encyclopedia of the Occult
    (Greer), 132
new-generation authors, 32–35
Newford books (de Lint), 9
Newman, Kim, 9, 50
Newsflesh series (Grant), 131
Niffenegger, Audrey, 130
Night of the Living Dead (pulp-era
    movie), 6–7, 136
Night of the Living Trekkies (Anderson),
    120
The Night of the Triffids (Clark), 85
Night Pleasures (Kenyon), ix
Nightmare on Elm Street, series (modern
    horror movies), 8
Niles, Steve, 133
nonfiction horror
    characteristics, 131–132
    titles, 132
Norman, Michael, 132
Northanger Abbey (Austen), 3
Nosferatu (silent film), 65
NoveList (database), 142
The Nymphos of Rocky Flats (Acevedo),
    120

O

Oates, Joyce Carol, 3, 129
occult. *See* witches and the occult
Ochse, Weston, 10, 80
Odd Thomas paranormal series
    (Koontz), 38
100 Wicked Little Witch Stories
    (Dziemianowicz, et al.), 104
Onions, Oliver, 5

P

pacing, horror and, 20
Pact of the Fathers (Campbell), 104
Paffenroth, Kim, 132
Pandemonium (Gregory), 115
paranormal *vs.* horror, 15–16
Pariah (Fingerman), 77
Partridge, Norman, 97
The Passage (Cronin), 16, 67
Passarella, J. G., 107

Paul is Undead (Goldsher), 122
Pawuk, Michael, 133
Pendle, George, 123–124
Penzler, Otto, 69
Peretti, Frank E., 97
Pendergast novels (Preston and Child), 131
Pet Sematary (King), 78
Phantom Nights (Farris), 60–61
phenomena, unexplainable (horror feature), 14
Piccirilli, Tom
  A Choir of Ill Children, 107
  major horror author, 9
  The Midnight Road, 131
Pinborough, Sarah
  Breeding Ground, 88
  major horror author of the 21st century, 10
  The Taken, 45, 62
  Tower Hill, 112, 117
Pine Deep trilogy (Maberry), 34–35
The Pines (Dunbar), 42, 95
Poe, Edgar Allen
  Edgar Allan Poe Audio Collection, 134
  ghost story author, 5
  key Gothic author, 3
  "The Tell-Tale Heart," 53
Poe's Children (Straub), 135
Polidori, John
  Gothic influence, 2
  key Gothic author, 3
Pratt, Tim, 117
The Presence (Saul), 97
Preston, Douglas
  Brimstone, 134
  Pendergast novels, 131
Prey (Crichton), 131
Price, E. Hoffman, 7
Price, Vincent, 6
Pride and Prejudice (Austen), ix, 122–123
Pride and Prejudice and Zombies (Grahame-Smith), 119–120, 122–123
Prime Evil (Winter), 135

psychological suspense
  characteristics, 128–129
  titles, 129
Pulliam, June Michele
  Hooked on Horror III, 50, 140
  Read On . . . Horror Fiction, 140

Q

Queen of Blood (Smith), 63
The Queen of the Damned (Rice), 70
Quirk Books, 119

R

RA for All: Horror (website), 141, 143
Radcliffe, Ann, 3
Ravenous (Garton), 86
The Reach (Kenyon), 116
Read On . . . Horror Fiction (Fonseca and Pulliam), 140
read-alike author pages, marketing and, 149–150
readers, matching books with, 27–29
readers' advisory department, marketing and, 149
The Readers' Advisory Guide to Graphic Novels (Goldsmith), 133
Readers' Advisory Service in the Public Library (Saricks), 18
The Reapers Are the Angels (Bell), 77, 129
Rebecca (du Maurier), 51
The Red Tree (Kiernan), 45, 86
Rendell, Ruth, 129
resources, horror, 139–144
Retro Pulp Tales series (Lansdale), 135
The Return (Little), 96
Rice, Anne
  ghost story author, 5
  Interview with a Vampire, 8, 16, 66
  key horror author, 9
  Mayfair Witches series, 107
  Vampire Chronicles, 70–71
  The Witching Hour, 102
The Ring (film), 136
Rise Against (Tripp), 81
The Rising (Keene), 41, 77–78
Rod Serling's Night Gallery (television series), 136

Rollins, James, 35, 131
Rollo, Gord, 117
Romero, George, 6
Rosemary's Baby (film), 136
Rosemary's Baby (Levin)
    classic horror, 53
    pulp-era movie, 7
Rot and Ruin (Maberry), 80
The Ruins (Smith), 30, 88–89, 90, 147
Rule, Ann, 132

S

Sacrifice (Everson), 104
'Salem's Lot (King), 68
Sandford, John, 38–39
Sandman series (Gaiman), 133
Saricks, Joyce, 18
Sarrantonio, Al, 135
Satan and demonic possession
    characteristics of, 111–113
    titles, 114–118
satirical frame, 26
Saul, John
    Black Creek Crossing, 107
    The Devil's Labyrinth, 117
    major horror author, 9
    Nathaniel, 62
    The Presence, 97
science, use in horror, 3–5
Scott, Beth, 132
Scream (comic horror movie), 119
Searcy, David, 97–98
Season of the Witch (Mostert), 106
serial killers *vs.* horror, 16
setting and frame, 22–23
Shannon, Harry, 10
Shapeshifter (Gonzalez), 86
shape-shifter stories
    characteristics of, 83–85
    titles, 85–90
Sharp Teeth (Barlow), 85
Shaun of the Dead (comic horror movie),
    119
She Wakes (Ketchum), 95
Shelley, Mary Wollstonecraft
    Frankenstein, 4, 53–54
    key Enlightenment author, 5

The Shining (King)
    classic horror, 36, 61
    film, 136
The Shore (Dunbar), 95
short story collections, 134–135
Sigler, Scott
    Ancestor, 98
    Infected, 134
    major horror author, 10
Simmons, Dan
    Drood, 134
    established horror authors,
        39–40
    major horror author, 9
    Song of Kali, 62
    Summer of Night, 62
    The Terror, 40, 47, 98
    A Winter Haunting, 62
Skipp, John, 10
Slade, Michael, 9
Slither (Lee), 87–88
Smith, Bryan
    Deathbringer, 80
    Depraved, 98
    House of Blood, 63
    major horror author, 10
    Queen of Blood, 63
    Soultaker, 88
Smith, Scott, 30, 88, 90, 129, 147
Snyder, Scott, 133
Sokoloff, Alexandra
    The Harrowing, 44, 63
    key Gothic author, 3
    key horror author, 10
    The Unseen, 23–26
    women horror writers, 43–44
Something Wicked This Way Comes
    (Bradbury), 50–51
Somtow, S. P., 80–81
Song of Kali (Simmons), 62
Sookie Stackhouse series, 9, 66
Soultaker (Smith), 88
Sparrow Rock (Kenyon), 17, 47, 78
Stableford, Brian, 9, 89
The Stand (King), 36
Stevenson, Robert Louis
    key Enlightenment author, 5

Stevenson, Robert Louis (cont.)
  *The Strange Case of Dr. Jekyll and Mr.
    Hyde*, 4, 54
Stoker, Bram
  Dracula, 4, 54
  key Enlightenment author, 5
  vampire book examples, 65–66
Stoker, Dacre, 71
The Stolen Child (Donohue), 134
The Stone Circle (Goshgarian), 104
Stories: All-New Tales (Gaiman and
    Sarrantonio), 135
story line, horror and, 21–22
Strain series (del Toro and Hogan),
    131
Strand, Jeff
  Benjamin's Parasite, 124
  Dweller, 46, 98
  major horror author, 10
  pulp horror, 42
The Strange Case of Dr. Jekyll and Mr. Hyde
    (Stevenson), 4, 54
The Stranger beside Me (Rule), 132
Stratford, Sarah Jane
  The Midnight Guardian, 71
  women horror authors, 45
Straub, Peter
  Black House, 46
  A Dark Matter, 108
  Floating Dragon, 98
  Ghost Story, 36–37, 47, 63
  major horror author, 9
  In the Night Room, 63
  Poe's Children, 135
  pulp horror, 36
  The Talisman, 47
Strieber, Whitley, 72, 89
style and language, horror and,
    20–21
Summer of Night (Simmons), 62
supernatural thriller
  characteristics of, 130–131
  titles, 131
Survivor (television series), 41
Swamp Thing series (Moore), 133
Sympathy for the Devil (Pratt), 117

T

The Taken (Pinborough), 45, 62
The Tale of the Body Thief (Rice), 70
Tales from the Crypt (television series),
    136
Tales from the Darkside (television series),
    136
Tales of Terror and Mystery (Doyle), 51
Tales of the Cthulhu Mythos (Lovecraft),
    135
The Talisman (King and Straub), 47
Taltos (Rice), 107
Taylor, Karen E., 31
Taylor, Terence, 72
television series and film, 136
"The Tell-Tale Heart" (Poe), 53
Templesmith, Ben, 133
terror (horror feature), 14
The Terror (Simmons), 40, 47, 98
themes, horror and, 21
*These Children Who Come at You with
    Knives* (Knipfel), 130
"Things That Go Bump in the Stacks," 15
13 Bullets: A Vampire Tale (Wellington), 72
13 Steps Down (Rendell), 129
30 Days of Night (Niles), 133
This Rage of Echoes (Clark), 94
The Tomb (Wilson), 39, 47
The Tommyknockers (King), 61
tone and mood, 18–19
Tower Hill (Pinborough), 112, 117
The Town (Little), 116
The Traveling Vampire Show (Laymon), 68
trends in horror, 26–27
Tripp, Ben, 81
The Turn of the Screw (James), 52, 57, 129
Turner, Joan Frances, 81
Twelve (Kent), 68
The Twilight Zone (television series),
    136
Twin Peaks (television series), 136

U

The Ultimate Witch (Preiss and
    Betancourt), 104
The Unseen (Sokoloff), 23–26, 63

V

The Vampire Archives (Penzler), 69
The Vampire Armand (Rice), 70
The Vampire Book (Melton), 132
The Vampire Lestat (Rice), 70
vampires
    characteristics of, 65–67
    titles, 67–74
The Vampyre (Polidori), 2
Vampyrrhic (Clark), 67
VanderMeer, Jeff, 130
Vaughan, Brian K., ix, 133

W

To Wake the Dead (Laymon), 96
The Walking Dead (Kirkman)
    graphic novels, 133
    television series, 136
    zombie novel, 78
Walpole, Horace
    The Castle of Otranto, 2, 54, 57
    key Gothic author, 3
Wandrei, Donald, 7
War for the Oaks (Bull), 130
Warner, Matthew, 140
Watchers (Koontz), 38, 47
Water Witch (LeBlanc), 105
Waters, Sarah, 129
Weinberg, Robert
    major horror author, 10
    100 Wicked Little Witch Stories, 104
    "What You Are Meant to Know," 50
Weird Tales (magazine), 53
Weird Times (magazine), 5
Wellington, David
    13 Bullets: A Vampire Tale, 72
    Frostbite, 89
    Monster trilogy, 81
Wells, H. G.
    ghost story author, 5
    The Invisible Man, 54–55
    The Island of Doctor Moreau, 4
    key Enlightenment author, 5
The Werewolves of London (Stableford), 89
Wharton, Edith, 5

"What You Are Meant to Know" (Weinberg), 10, 50
Whitby Vampyrrhic (Clark), 67
Whitehead, Henry S., 7
whole collection readers' advisory, 127–128
Wildwood Road (Golden), 114–115
Wilson, F. Paul
    established horror author, 39
    major horror author, 9
    Midnight Mass, 72
    The Tomb, 39
Winter, Douglas, 13, 135
A Winter Haunting (Simmons), 62
The Witch (Mitchell), 106
Witch Wood (Buchan), 103
witches and the occult
    characteristics of, 101–103
    titles, 103–109
The Witching Hour (Rice), 102, 107
Wither (Passarella), 107
The Wolf Man (pulp-era movie), 6
The Wolfman (Maberry), 99
The Wolf's Hour (McCammon), 88
Wolf's Trap (Gagliani), 85–86
Women of the Otherworld series (Armstrong), 17, 130
Wong, David, 124
The Woods Are Dark (Laymon), 96
World War Z (Brooks), 77, 134
Wormwood: Gentleman Corpse series (Templesmith), 133
Wuthering Heights (Brontë), 3, 51, 57
Wyatt, Neal, 127

Y

Y: The Last Man series (Vaughn), 133
Yarbro, Chelsea Quinn, 9
You Come When I Call You (Clegg), 94
You Don't Scare Me (Farris), 95
You Suck (Moore), 119

Z

Zeltserman, Dave, 89
Zombie (Oates), 129

zombie books
    characteristics of, 75–76
    titles, 76–82
The Zombies of Lake Woebegotten (Geillor),
    122
The Zombie Survival Guide (Brooks), 132

zombies *vs.* horror, 17
zombies *vs.* vampires, 26
zombify website, 76